STEVEN L. CASE

GOD UP CLOSE

12 Full-Contact Encounters with God

PARTICIPANT'S GUIDE

youth specialties

ZONDERVAN.com/
AUTHORTRACKER
follow your favorite authors

ZONDERVAN

God Up Close Participant's Guide: 12 Full-Contact Encounters with God
Copyright © 2010 by Steven L. Case

YS Youth Specialties is a trademark of YOUTHWORKS!, INCORPORATED and is registered with the United States Patent and Trademark Office.

Requests for information should be addressed to:
Zondervan, Grand Rapids, Michigan 49530

ISBN 978-0-310-67044-5

All Scripture quotations, unless otherwise indicated, are taken from the Holy Bible, *Today's New International Version*™. *TNIV*®. Copyright 2001, 2005 by Biblica, Inc.™ Used by permission of Zondervan. All rights reserved worldwide.

Any Internet addresses (websites, blogs, etc.) and telephone numbers printed in this book are offered as a resource. They are not intended in any way to be or imply an endorsement by Zondervan, nor does Zondervan vouch for the content of these sites and numbers for the life of this book.

All rights reserved. No part of this publication may be reproduced, stored in a retrieval system, or transmitted in any form or by any means—electronic, mechanical, photocopy, recording, or any other—except for brief quotations in printed reviews, without the prior permission of the publisher.

Cover and interior design: SharpSeven Design

Printed in the United States of America

10 11 12 13 14 15 /DCI/ 23 22 21 20 19 18 17 16 15 14 13 12 11 10 9 8 7 6 5 4 3 2 1

CONTENTS

INTRODUCTION	5
JACOB	9
ABRAHAM AND ISAAC	19
STORMS	29
THE MAN BORN BLIND	39
DANIEL	49
ELIJAH	61
EZEKIEL	71
JOB	81
MARY MAGDALENE	91
SAUL/PAUL	101
CORNELIUS AND PETER	111
BEZALEL	121

INTRODUCTION

Let's learn some Hebrew. Just you and me. It will take just a minute.

Let's start with this word:

Transliterated it reads like this: *Chay* (or *Chayah*).

Pronounced it sounds like this: khah'ee.

Imagine you're saying the word *Hi*. Give the "h" a little bit of phlegm in the back of your throat. (Someone once said Hebrew is the language of coughing and spitting.)

Now give the "e" sound an extra beat: Hi-ee.

Practice that once or twice.

Now let's move on.

Try this one:

אלהי

Fire up the transliteration machine and we get this: *'Elohiym*.

Pronounce it like this: El-o-heem'.

Imagine you're saying "Hello." Drop the "h" and you get "ello." Now say "heem" (rhymes with "seem").

Ello-heem.

Now let's put it all together:

Chay Elohiym
khah'ee el-o-heem'
Hi-ee Ello-heem

It's one of the many names for God in the Bible. David used it when he accepted the challenge of the giant in 1 Samuel 17:45. He used it again in his psalms: "My soul thirsts for _____" (63:1). "I will sing praise to _____" (104:33).

The prophet Isaiah used those words to talk about the God who was connected to all things (Isaiah 37:4, 17). It appears in the New Testament as a word for Jesus (Colossians 2:9). It's also used in Titus 2:13 to describe God in the church.

It means "God alive."

Not God IS alive (that was sort of a given) but God alive.

Elohiym is a God who is fully God. Big. Universal. The Creator of all that is and all that was and all that will ever be. Massive God. Eternal God. Bigger-than-your-mind-can-conceive God. Imagine the word being spoken by James Earl Jones in that wonderful, deep, rich, resonant voice.

GOD.

Now let's look at *chay*.

Alive. Fully alive. *Chay* is how you feel when you step off the world's tallest, fastest, steepest roller coaster. *Chay* is the "alive" you feel at the end of a great concert. It's the "alive" you feel when the weather is just right and the highway is open and the windows are down and the perfect song comes on the radio.

ALIVE.

Have you ever leaned too far back in your chair and felt that brief moment of "Ahhhh!!"? Imagine THAT, only in a good way. That's the "alive" we're talking about.

GOD	-	ALIVE
Giant	-	Roller Coaster
Creator	-	Third Encore
James Earl Jones' Voice	-	Driving with the Windows Open

That's the God we're going to get to know in these pages.

This is a book of stories about people who met God—up close. These are stories about a full-on connection to *Chay Elohiym*.

They're all based on stories from the Bible. Dramatized? Sure. Real? Absolutely. Of all the words we can use to describe God, *distant* isn't one of them. God is here, now. God is in this moment, as you read these words.

God is here.

Above. Below. Beside. Beneath. Behind. Before.

God is here.

Within. Embracing. Inspiring. Encompassing. Pouring. Enveloping.

God is here.

God is.

God was.

God always will be.

Okay? Now let's tell some stories.

JACOB

Based on Genesis 32:22-31

Jacob squatted in silence by the fire. Yesterday the camp had been alive with the sounds of children playing and women shooing them away from the fire. Away from Jacob. The women—Jacob's two wives and their servants—knew to keep the children away whenever he got like this.

Jacob loved his children with all his heart, loved them as much as he loved anything. But when they were rambunctious and full of vinegar, he'd snap at them and they'd cry. Then he'd hold them and whisper gently, "It's okay. Daddy's sorry," until one of the women came to take them away. That's what the camp was like when Jacob was thinking about things, when he was deep in himself.

And that's why he'd sent the entire camp—his wives, his children, the servants, and the animals—away. They'd taken the tents and left him alone by the fire with his bedroll. Jacob poked a stick at the wood in the flames. It wasn't worry that kept him awake. And it wasn't the fear that his brother might very well kill him tomorrow. It was the thought of facing his brother at all. The brother he'd cheated out of the family inheritance. The brother he'd left behind to care for the family business while he took the money and ran.

Esau.

Jacob had thought about his brother almost every day. The way Esau had shouted from the top of the mountain when he realized that not only was the inheritance gone, but so was Jacob.

His brother was a big man. He'd also been a big boy. When they were children, their mother used to say they'd fought with each other inside her belly, too, and she had to sing to get them to calm down and let her rest.

When they were boys, Esau was always the stronger and faster one. He used to push Jacob down and throw rotten fruit at him. His aim was perfect. He was merciless. When he was eight, Esau was already bringing home animals for their mother to cook. It was usually some bird or deer he'd beaned with a rock and then killed with his bare hands. Their father, Isaac, would laugh, put his hand on Esau's shoulder, and tell Esau he was proud of his firstborn. Firstborn by mere minutes, mind you. But firstborn was firstborn. That was the way of their people.

Esau would look at his father and smile. Those looks annoyed Jacob at first. In time, he grew to hate them.

So Jacob had done what he'd done. He'd posed as Esau, tricked his blind father, and stolen the blessing that should have gone to his brother. Then he'd run away and started a new life. Years later the voice of God told Jacob he had to go home. He had to heal the rift with his brother. He had to atone, amend, apologize.

Jacob had sent his wives and children ahead with gifts for Esau. Word had come back that Esau had gathered an army of 400 men and would be standing at the end of the field where the brothers once played as children. Tomorrow, Jacob would walk into that field alone. He'd kneel before his older brother and beg his forgiveness.

Jacob stared into the fire. He was no longer the young man who'd spent all his time studying. He was no longer the man who, with the help of his mother, had deceived his father and cheated his brother. That man was gone. That man had become someone else. The years of working for his father-in-law had made Jacob a different person.

Jacob was so deep in thought that he didn't hear the stranger arrive. The stranger was so silent that Jacob didn't know he was near until he saw the man sitting on his haunches with his arms resting on his knees, just as Jacob was doing, staring into the flames.

The man looked up just as Jacob did. Their eyes met, and the man seemed to smile, although Jacob couldn't be sure. The stranger tilted his head the way a child does when he ponders a strange new flower or animal. The man across the fire had no beard. He had no lines on his face. Jacob would have guessed him to be no more than a teenager, but for the sheer size of him. He was bigger than Jacob remembered Esau being. Jacob slowly moved his hand from his knee to the handle of the scabbard tied to his belt.

The stranger's smile widened, as though he knew exactly what Jacob was doing. The man's teeth were white and perfect. The fire reflected in his eyes in a way that fascinated and disturbed Jacob. The hair that spilled from beneath the man's turban was pure white. His clothes were the same as any other man's, but Jacob saw they were clean—no, not clean…new. It was as if this perfect man had suddenly come into existence in an instant.

Jacob had long ago stopped being surprised by such happenings in his life. "Who are you?" he asked.

The man—the "new" man who squatted across the fire from him—continued to smile, and then he tilted his head to the other side as if he were apprising Jacob.

"Who *are* you?" Jacob asked again. Still there was no answer. The man's eyes glistened in the firelight.

Jacob had had enough. He was cold. He was tired. He'd spent the past few days packing up his wives and children. He'd spent the past few nights picturing the many ways his older brother might kill him. And now some alabaster-faced man-child was playing games with him in the middle of the night. It was too much.

Jacob stood and reached for his scabbard. But before he could draw the blade, the man jumped to his feet and leaped over the flames at Jacob. He put two marble-white hands on Jacob's shoulders and forced him to the ground. Jacob went down on his back. Hard. The knife tumbled away from him, out of range of the fire's glow. Jacob scrambled to his feet and looked around. The stranger was gone.

Jacob stood still. Listening. Listening the way he did when he and his brother used to play hiding games as boys. Esau was too big and dense to be perfectly quiet, so Jacob always found him immediately. Now Jacob listened but heard nothing…until the man rushed at him from the left, pushed him to the ground again, and disappeared into the dark.

When the man leaped out of the darkness and into the firelight a third time, Jacob nearly shouted. The man had wings.

Wings.

Greater than those of a hawk. Longer than the tent Jacob shared with Rachel. Wider than his camels when they stood side by side. The stranger had *wings*.

The stranger shoved him to the ground yet again. This time Jacob landed on his back, which forced all the air from his lungs. He gasped, trying to breathe in, but all he could do was breathe out. Finally his lungs settled and he began to breathe normally.

The stranger stepped out of the darkness and into the light of the fire. The wings were tucked behind him, but Jacob could see they were higher than the giant man's head. Jacob looked the stranger in the eye and held out his hand to be lifted up. The stranger stepped forward and grabbed Jacob's hand, but Jacob yanked the man forward and planted both feet in his rib cage. In one smooth motion, Jacob rolled backward and flipped the man over his head. The stranger landed far enough away that the dying fire didn't illuminate him. Then Jacob heard him laugh.

It wasn't an evil laugh. It was more like a child's laugh coming from a man's throat. The stranger was having fun.

"WHO ARE YOU?" Jacob shouted at the darkness. But the question was moot. Jacob already knew he was in the presence of one of God's messengers. And this one liked to wrestle.

Jacob knew that as long as he stood in the light of the fire, he was at a disadvantage. He was the only one who could be seen. It was time to make things a little more equal. Jacob scooped up two handfuls of sand and tossed them on the flames. The dark was almost instantaneous.

"This is how God answers my prayers?" Jacob said to the darkness.

This time he heard the steps. He heard the flap of the wings that lifted the stranger into the air when the sound of his footsteps stopped. He wasn't caught by surprise. He felt the front of the angel's new robe and pulled them both to the ground.

They wrestled in the dirt and dust until the sun began to break over the horizon. They both turned and looked at the growing light. In the dim, Jacob was able to grab the angel and force him to the ground. He put a knee on the being's chest and pinned him there.

The being spoke for the first time. "It is dawn. I must go."

Jacob looked at him. He'd beaten an angel. There was no blood on the stranger. His clothes still looked new. Jacob, on the other hand, could taste his own blood and the dirt in his mouth. But he knew he'd beaten one of God's angels.

"My God has sent you to me with a blessing," Jacob said. "You will give it to me now."

The angel smiled.

Jacob grabbed him by the front of his tunic and yanked him forward so they were nearly touching noses.

"YOU WILL GIVE ME MY BLESSING."

"What is your name?" the angel asked.

"My name is Jacob."

The angel reached out and, with no more effort than a man picks a blade of grass, touched Jacob's hip. Immediately Jacob's hip bone popped out of its socket.

Jacob howled in pain and fell forward. The stranger pushed Jacob off him letting him roll onto his back. Screaming at the searing pain that shot up and down his side, Jacob clutched his hip and tried to pound the bone back into place.

As the sun cleared the horizon, Jacob looked up and saw the face of the angel clearly for the first time. "Who are you?" he asked.

The angel bent low and replied, "Why would you want to know my name?"

He put his hand on Jacob's face and brushed the sweaty, filthy hair from his eyes. Jacob met the angel's eyes and in that moment felt no pain.

The angel said, "You have wrestled enough. It is time to go home. This is God's blessing. Your name is no longer Jacob. From this moment on, you are Israel."

The angel disappeared and the searing pain returned. Jacob, now Israel, screamed again. He pounded on his hip bone, which was visible through his robe. On the third try, he felt the bone slide back into its socket. The intense blinding pain subsided and became a dull ache that embedded itself deep inside Jacob's hip. It was an ache he'd feel for the rest of his life.

Lying on his back in the dirt, Jacob waited until the sun was fully up before he tried to move. He rolled onto his stomach, managed to get on all fours, and then stood. His first step sent a pain from his bruised hip throughout his entire body. The second step was easier. Then the next. He limped toward the horizon.

His name was Israel.

Last night he'd wrestled with an angel of God.

Today he'd meet his brother who'd likely kill him and then take his wives and children and all of his treasure.

Nothing surprised him anymore.

RANDOM THOUGHTS ABOUT THE STORY OF JACOB

We all have broken relationships in our lives—friendships that were torn apart, resentments buried deep in our souls that were never resolved. At some point we have to fix things. We have to make amends.

List five things that are broken in your life—anything from mp3 players to relationships. Jot them down in the order of the length of time they've been broken.

After the wrestling match, two name changes took place. The angel changed Jacob's name to Israel, which in Hebrew means, "one who has struggled with God." Later, Jacob changed the name of the land where the wrestling match took place. He called it *Peniel*, which means "face of God."

Jacob demands two things of the angel: To know his name and to receive a blessing from God. If you know someone's name, you have a certain amount of control over that person. You can shout, "Hey, Bob!" in a crowded mall or ballpark and anyone named Bob will turn to see who called. When Moses went before God, he said, "Who do I say sent me?" He was asking God for his name. God simply replied, "Tell them I AM sent you."

What is the origin of your name? Is it a family name? Do you know its meaning? Look up the meaning of your name and write it here.

Many sermons and hymns are about asking God to rain down his blessings upon us. The idea is that we'll stand with our hands up, ready to catch the blessings as they fall from the sky. Not Jacob. Jacob fought for his blessings. Can't you picture him grabbing an angel of God by the front of his shirt and saying, "Give me my blessing!"?

Cast this scene as though it were a movie. Who would play the angel? Who would play Jacob?

This was Jacob's life-changing moment—and he knew it. He was going to take his moment, rather than let it come to him. How often do we stand back and wonder where God is? How often do we assume God is ignoring us or leaving us alone simply because we haven't received anything from our prayer list? God is not Santa. God is God. Very often the blessings are right in front of us, but we're too caught up in ourselves or our rules or the lives of others that we fail to grab them.

THE STORY CONTINUES

In those days, people believed that certain areas of your body controlled certain emotions. The pelvic area controlled pride. Essentially Jacob had to have his pride dislocated before he could make amends with his brother. What needs to be dislocated in you? What are you holding on to that may be keeping you from healing a broken relationship? Write down one thing, one small micro-movement that may start you on the journey to reconciliation. Try to accomplish that small step forward this week.

ABRAHAM AND ISAAC

Based on Genesis 22:1-19

Abraham made sure he had two skins of water, a bag of figs, and enough dried meat and unleavened bread for two. He hoped he wouldn't have to eat in front of his son, Isaac, because there was no way he'd be able to keep his food down. And Isaac couldn't know anything was wrong.

Abraham seriously thought about not going back. It would be easier than going back alone. Eventually Sarah would assume they were *both dead*. She'd grieve for a few months, and then she'd take the others to live with her sister. She'd never have to know what he'd done.

Why would God ask this of him? What kind of loving father would ask such a thing? Abraham covered the donkey's back with a riding blanket and leaned his head against the animal's spine. For a moment he was overwhelmed by what he was going to do, and he choked on his tears.

Hearing his wife coming up behind him, he stood and wiped his eyes. She must not see him this way. Dear God, what was he going to tell Sarah? How do you explain something like that to your wife?

She put her hand on his shoulder, and he turned to face her. "What's wrong?" she asked. She knew him so well.

"Nothing."

"Abraham," she said like she always did.

He smiled and stared at her face—the face he'd watched in moments of joy and pain. How could he say the words to her?

"He's growing up so quickly," Abraham said. "Sometimes I look at him and I wonder—"

Sarah ran her fingers through his beard. "He is his father's child," she said. "I see so much of you in him. Your taking him along today means so much."

Isaac emerged from their simple tent. He had the walking stick his father had carved for him. It was too big for his hand, but Abraham had told him he'd grow into it. He'd also draped his father's hand-me-down shawl over his shoulders. He wanted so much to be a man in his father's eyes, but the staff and shawl made him look all the more like a child. He was being very serious about the trip. His father had told him he was going along to worship God, to make the sacrifice.

Sarah resisted the urge to cry and run over to hold Isaac's face in her hands. Abraham could sense her hesitation and wished she *would* run to her son. She'd want that memory. She wasn't going to understand. How could she? *He* didn't understand.

Isaac approached his parents, and in his most serious tone he said, "I'm ready to go, Father."

Abraham nodded and said, "Good. Kiss your mother and we'll be off."

Isaac looked at Abraham as if to say, *I'm not a child.*

Abraham looked back at Isaac and nodded his head solemnly, as if to say, *Yes, you* will *kiss your mother goodbye.*

For just a moment, there was a trace of a stubborn, childlike I'm-not-going-to-eat-my-vegetables look in Isaac's eyes. Abraham bent low and said, "You will kiss your mother goodbye. It's what a man does."

Isaac blinked and pulled his gaze away from his father's face. Then he walked over and placed a gentle peck on his mother's cheek. Sarah looked at Abraham over the top of Isaac's head as though they were sharing a secret. Abraham thought his wife knew nothing of secrets. She was going to hate him when he returned. She'd refuse to speak to him for the rest of his life. She was a stubborn woman and could probably manage it, too. Then again, what he had to do—what he'd been asked to do—would probably kill her.

He looked at her face and then quickly looked at the ground. If she saw his eyes, she'd know he was keeping something from her. He looked at the sky as if checking the weather. Then he wrapped his arms around his wife and hugged her tightly.

"Oh!" she laughed. He hadn't lifted her off the ground in a long time. He planted a loving kiss on her lips, and she kissed him back. She didn't know where this sudden affection was coming from, but she wanted to enjoy it.

ABRAHAM AND ISAAC

Abraham cinched the rope around the donkey's belly and lifted his son onto the animal's back.

"I want to walk," Isaac said.

"No, no," Abraham said gently. "You can ride on the way there, and I'll ride on the way back. How does that sound to you?"

Isaac nodded as if he'd just bartered for a field of crops or a wife. Either way it was a great negotiation. Sarah waved as they started down the path. These were her two men, going off together to make a sacrifice to the Lord. She felt proud.

The place where God told Abraham to sacrifice his son was a three-day journey. On the way they ate dates and filled their skins from the stream. Abraham took every opportunity to touch his boy, to put a hand on his back, to tussle his hair. Isaac instinctively pulled away. Men didn't do those things. He thought his father was treating him like a child. In truth, it was all Abraham could do not to scoop the boy into his arms and hold him like he'd done when Isaac was a toddler.

"Father?" Isaac said when they were nearly to the place of sacrifice.

"Yes?"

"We have the wood and the coals. You have your knife. Where is the lamb for the sacrifice?"

Abraham didn't look back. He couldn't. He choked on his words but only for a moment. "The Lord will provide, boy. The Lord always provides."

They reached a clearing on the mountain, and Abraham helped his son off the donkey. "I don't think I brought enough wood," he said. "I need you to find some more so our fire will be big and the Lord will see the smoke from his throne in heaven. Go get us some more wood. Off with you now."

Isaac launched himself away, glad to be off the mule and eager to help his father build the altar.

When he was gone, Abraham looked at the sky. "Why?" he asked quietly. "This is what a loving God demands? This is what you want? Why? His mother waited so long!"

When there was no answer, Abraham gritted his teeth. He felt an anger growing inside him. "This is what you want? To give us this miracle and then take it away? What's the purpose? Why didn't you just leave us childless? This is too much." He waited. Then, without meaning to, he shouted, "Answer me!!"

"I'm right here, Father," Isaac called back. He came around the curve of the path, his arms loaded with sticks. He was trying to carry too many and dropped some of them, leaving a trail of twigs and leaves behind him.

"Oh, that's my good son," Abraham said. "That will make a nice fire. And look, I've found two rocks for the altar."

For the next hour, Abraham and Isaac fashioned the altar table from the sticks and reeds Isaac had found. Abraham's old fingers guided his son's little ones as they tied the branches together. Abraham did all he could to delay finishing the job because he knew that once the altar was finished, there'd be only one thing left to do. Yet Isaac grew impatient.

Finally, the two of them set the altar between the two rocks. Isaac grabbed the coals and the extra wood and began to prepare the fire beneath the altar table.

"Has God provided the lamb yet?" he asked as he leaned the sticks onto the coals.

"My flints are in the saddlebag," Abraham said. "Run and fetch them."

Isaac sprang away toward the mule. Abraham looked at the sky one last time. "Please." It was a plea. He swallowed his rage and sorrow and smiled at Isaac as he returned with the flint rocks in his hand. "Good boy."

"Now then," Abraham said, "we need to find this lamb God is sending to us. Have you seen one?"

Isaac shook his head. He hadn't been looking.

"Well, I'm quite sure there's one around," Abraham said. "I thought I heard it, but my old eyes can't see. Come here." Abraham reached down and lifted his son onto the altar. He kissed the back of Isaac's head, lightly, so the boy wouldn't turn around.

"Look off toward the west, just there. Is that a ram?"

"I don't see anything," Isaac replied.

"Look hard. I'm sure it's there."

Abraham unsheathed his knife and held it behind his back.

"Father, I don't—"

"*Look*," Abraham insisted. "Look very hard. I think it's waaaaay up there on the rock. You see it, don't you?"

Isaac squinted and Abraham forced himself to thrust the blade toward his son's neck.

Before the knife got near the boy's skin, a hand wrapped itself around Abraham's wrist and held it firmly in midair.

Abraham turned and saw the angel.

It was massive—much larger than the men in white who'd come to his home years earlier. This angel was twice Abraham's size. Its long white hair hung down on either side of its face. Its wings covered all three of them. Sheltered them. Cocooned them in warmth and peace. Abraham felt one hand on his wrist and another on his shoulder. A sudden warmth ran through his body—a warmth he'd never known. It was love. It was pure. It was shalom.

The angel leaned in and whispered in his ear, "Don't hurt the boy. God says let him live. God was testing you, and now he knows how much you love him."

The giant messenger of God vanished, and an overwhelming sense of relief washed over Abraham. Abraham dropped the knife and clutched his son to his chest. "Ohhhh, my boy, my boy," he said as he kissed his son's head.

"Father," Isaac said in an exasperated voice, "I saw the ram."

"What?" Abraham asked. He was crying now.

Isaac pulled back to look at his father. "What's wrong?" he asked.

Abraham wiped the tears from his eyes. "The sun," he replied. "I told you it's too much for these old eyes of mine. Now where is this ram you saw?"

"Just there," Isaac said and pointed.

Abraham turned and saw on the next ledge a fat young ram with its horns caught in a thicket.

Isaac smiled at his father. "The Lord will provide." He jumped to the ground and ran toward the trapped animal.

"And the Lord cuts it close sometimes," Abraham said. He looked at the sky and whispered, "Thank you," and walked after his son.

RANDOM THOUGHTS ABOUT THE STORY OF ABRAHAM AND ISAAC

This is one of the most difficult stories in Scripture. The immediate question that arises is "Why? Why would God ask such a thing?" God knew Abraham was faithful enough to sacrifice his son. God also knew he'd never let Abraham hurt a hair on the boy's head. But Abraham didn't know that. So the second question that arises is "Could *I* show that kind of faithfulness?"

For a million dollars, would you throw the switch of an electric chair and execute someone? Would you be willing to give up everything you own if you knew it would spare the life of a child in the poorest section of Haiti?

In the Introduction we learned the phrase for "God alive" (*Chay Elohiym*). In this story Abraham calls God *Yireh Elohiym*, which means "God provides." In other words God will give you what you need. More than that, though, the name refers to God's eye affecting his heart. What God sees makes a difference in what God does.

What do you *need*? (You'll notice we didn't ask, "What do you *want*?") Make a short list of your needs here.

A life of faith is not an easy life.

To say, "This doesn't make sense," is the wrong line of thinking. To "make sense" of something is to rely on the senses. Can I touch it, taste it, see it, hear it, or smell it? Faith simply means to rely on something *more* than our senses.

Do you believe there are a bazillion stars in the universe? How do you know if you've never seen them all? Do you believe it when someone says, "I love you"? What proof do you need?

Abraham probably had a three-day walk in which to ponder what he was going to do. He had three days to turn around and go home. He had every chance to throw that blade away. But he didn't.

He didn't.

Ultimately, Abraham did exactly what God asked of him. Obedience hurts. But in the end, God provided (*Yireh Elohiym*).

You know when your curfew is, and you know what will happen if you break it. As fun as the party may be, as good as that conversation is...we still go home. When you decide to be obedient, sometimes your parents cut you some slack the next time.

Think of a common, everyday example of obedience being rewarded in your life. Write it here.

So it is with God.

God doesn't sit on a throne with his "Naughty or Nice?" list and keep track of all that we do, just waiting for us to mess up. God watches. God sees and it affects his heart.

What we do affects our lives.

God sees. God provides.

Say that last part out loud.

God sees. God provides.

Your relationship with God works like a conversation.

Listen. Speak. Learn. Live. Enjoy.

THE STORY CONTINUES

Make a list of things you do exceptionally well. Your list might include things like painting, drawing, working with kids, encouraging others, math, music, sports and more. How might God use your skills for his glory or to help someone in need? How might you sing for God? How might you tutor someone for God? How might you offer encouragement to someone who's down? Do that this week.

STORMS

Based on Mark 4:35–5:20 and Luke 8:22-39

Jesus loved the sea. He liked to walk alongside it in the mornings. He liked to relax near it on hot afternoons. He loved the feeling of water cascading over his head and the silence that enveloped him beneath the waves. He liked to walk and play on the beach with his friends. And he had a unique ability to splash only those people that he believed needed to get wet.

The disciples learned to walk behind Jesus when they were with him on the shore because anyone who walked beside or in front of him ran the risk of having a cold wave of water splash onto his back. Inevitably, the recipient of the splash would spin around only to find Jesus sauntering with his hands clasped behind his back, gazing up at the clouds, and whistling.

The seashore was where Jesus recruited several of his disciples. He loved to teach there more than at any other place—even the temple or people's homes, which had too many distractions. But there was something about the continuous sound of the waves coming ashore that made people relax, sit back, and listen.

One day, after a very long morning of teaching and healing, Jesus was walking on the same beach where he'd first met Peter and Andrew. Their family's fishing boat was sitting on the shore. But this was more than a rowboat. It easily had room for all 12 disciples. Jesus saw the boat and smiled.

"We're going to the other side of the lake," he said and started to run for the boat.

They all pushed the boat into the water and climbed aboard. Jesus settled himself on the fishing nets and breathed deeply as the sea wind blew through his hair and beard. "Ahhhhhhhhhhhh-hhhhhh," he said quietly. He was soon fast asleep.

Those disciples who'd been fishermen before they chose to follow Jesus assembled the sail while the others rowed. Matthew, who was a tax collector by trade and a numbers guy from birth, simply clung to the side and eventually "brought forth" what he was sure was the majority of the leftover fish and bread. Peter, Andrew, James, and John all laughed at him and his peculiar shade of green. He sat up as the others smirked at him.

"Laugh now," Matthew said. "But I'll be waiting for you when it's time to do your taxes." They all laughed again—all except Jesus who made a small "yip" noise and dreamed more deeply.

Peter saw the storm coming first. An experienced fisherman, he knew how to keep a trained eye on the horizon. But this storm came out of nowhere. There were no clouds in the distance. There was no smell of rain on the breeze. He saw the storm just moments before it was upon them.

"Hang on!" was all he could manage to say before it hit them full force. The waves dropped out from under them, pitching the boat forward and backward. The disciples managed to get the sail down just before a giant wave washed over the side of the boat. James and John took the ropes from the sail and tied themselves to the mast. Matthew, who was clutching the side of the boat as tightly as he could, leaned over and threw up again. A few others joined him. Jesus didn't move.

Thaddeus crawled on all fours to the front of the boat where the Savior lay sleeping. "Uh... Jesus?" he said.

"Mmmmmmmmmm?" Jesus mumbled.

"Hey, Jesus? We're all gonna die here!" Thad yelled.

Jesus opened his eyes and saw the water dripping off the face of the disciple who couldn't grow a decent beard. He saw the fear in the young man's eyes. Standing up, he opened his arms and allowed the rain to drench him. Turning around, he saw his 12 disciples holding on to each other and whatever else might keep them inside the boat. Jesus started to laugh.

Turning back to the storm, Jesus put a finger to his lips and said, "Shhhhhhhhhhhh-hhhhhhhhhhhhh."

Immediately the storm stopped and the sea became as smooth as glass.

Jesus turned back to the dripping disciples who now looked very silly still tied to the mast. Jesus sat on an overturned bucket and asked, "What was the last thing I said before we got into the boat?"

The disciples looked at each other and then back at Jesus.

Jesus rolled his eyes. "Didn't I say we were going to the other side?"

The disciples looked at each other again and then back at Jesus. They nodded.

"Oh, good," Jesus said, "then I wasn't talking to myself. If the Son of God says, 'We're going to the other side of the lake,' do you believe there's *anything* in heaven or earth that could prevent us from getting there? Where's your faith?"

Unfortunately the disciples missed the point. They were more astonished that Jesus had just shushed a storm. "That was the coolest trick ever," they whispered.

Now the boat pulled into shore at Gerasenes, a town where good Jewish boys didn't hang out. Jesus stepped out of the boat and began to walk along the beach with his feet in the water. The still-soggy-but-quickly-drying disciples pulled the boat onto the beach and ran after him.

As they walked past a cemetery, they heard a noise. At first it sounded like an animal. But as they got closer, they began to make out words. It sounded as if a lion or bear had acquired the ability to speak.

As the words became clear, the disciples looked at each other. Though most of them had never been this far from home, they knew those words. They distinctly heard words you didn't say around your mother, no matter how old you were. And the only thing more shocking than the words themselves was the appearance of the person speaking them.

Running around in that cemetery was the largest human being they'd ever seen. And the fact that he hadn't had a haircut or shaved in years made him look like a wild creature. The man also happened to be naked.

The people of the town had long since forgotten his name. To them, he was just the crazy naked guy who yelled at tombstones. On several occasions they'd tried to chain him down for his own good. (He had a tendency to hit himself in the head with rocks and cut his skin.) But every time he somehow managed to break the chains and returned to the cemetery to shout obscenities at people no one else could see. The town ignored him. He was crazy—but he was *their* crazy.

The man spotted Jesus and the disciples and ran toward them. He roared like an animal. Chains hung from his wrists, remnants of the townspeople's most recent attempt to control him. The veins on his neck bulged as he screamed something incoherent.

Jesus looked up at the man who towered over him and said, "Shhhhhhhhhhhhhhhhhhhhhh."

The man stopped screaming and fell to his knees, weeping like a child.

"What are you doing here?" Jesus asked.

In a gravelly voice, the man said, "I can't take it."

"What?"

The man pressed the heels of his hands over his eyes. "Voices," he said.

Jesus looked at the man as if he were a parent examining a child's scraped knee. "Is that why you cut yourself? To let the voices out?"

The man didn't look at Jesus, but he nodded.

"Do they talk to you?"

The man held his head as if he were trying to keep it from exploding. He nodded again.

"Do they have names?" There was something more serious in Jesus' voice now.

"There are so many," the man said.

Jesus brushed the hair out of the big man's face. The fog that had kept the man isolated for so long suddenly lifted; for the first time in his life, he could think clearly. He began to weep. He leaned forward and sobbed on Jesus' shoulder. He cried for his lost years. He cried for his lost family. He cried in fear about what to do next. Suddenly he stood up and said to Jesus, "Let me come with you. I'll clean myself up. You look like you could use a bouncer."

Jesus smiled. "No. You need to stay here. Go home. Show yourself to your friends and family. Tell them what happened. You could have a career in youth ministry."

The giant of a man shook his head as if trying to make the voices come back. For a moment he was frightened. "Where did they all go?"

Jesus' reply was interrupted by a screaming, screeching, wailing noise. Everyone jumped as a herd of pigs, squealing in agony, burst through the brush and ran onto the beach. But the pigs didn't stop at the water's edge. They all ran into the sea where they drowned within minutes. The disciples looked at Jesus. Jesus looked at the disciples. The disciples looked at the large, hairy, naked man. The large, hairy, naked man looked at the herd of dead swine floating in the surf. Everyone looked back at Jesus.

Jesus said, "What?"

The man left the cemetery and bathed. He cut his hair. He shaved and put on new clothes. He cleaned up real nice. Then he went back to his hometown to tell people what happened. But the people were afraid of him. They couldn't see anything but the crazy man who'd lived with the dead. They went to Jesus and asked, "Why did you have to come and mess with the way things are?"

Jesus pointed to the man and said, "Look at him. He's no longer naked. He's no longer living in a cemetery. He's not cutting himself with rocks."

"Things were fine the way they were," the people said.

"He's been healed for God's sake," Jesus pointed out.

"Maybe you should go," the people replied. "There's a way things are and a way they're going to be."

Jesus and the disciples climbed back into their boat, and again the once-crazy man begged to go with them. Jesus smiled and said, "I'm telling you, youth ministry. You're a natural."

So the man stayed and pursued a career in youth ministry, and he did quite well.

RANDOM THOUGHTS ABOUT THE STORY OF JESUS SHUSHING THE STORMS

Did Jesus *really* tell the formerly scary naked man to go into youth ministry?

No. But can you think of a better career choice? Seriously, who else but young people would listen to the guy?

When you need to drive somewhere, are you more likely to trust your GPS, an online map site, or someone who's made the same journey many times before?

These two stories show us Jesus' power. He shushed the storm and shushed the voices in the man's head. Jesus calms storms—of all kinds.

Out in the boat, the disciples hung on for dear life. And so did the crazy naked guy living among the tombs. In many ways we're *all* just hanging on for dear life.

Draw a picture of yourself on a boat in a storm. Are you hanging over the side, barfing? Are you lashing yourself to the mast? Are you trying to steer in the midst of a hopeless situation?

Label the storm based on the things that are trying to wreck your life right now. Give names to the wind, rain and rough seas.

Jesus told the man to stay. The crowds were angry, so they told Jesus and his disciples to leave, which they did. But the crowds couldn't stop the story. They had a living, breathing example of God's power right in front of them. They couldn't ignore it.

Sometimes we get the idea that we have to be a certain kind of person or live a certain kind of life in order to be an effective messenger of God's love. Truthfully, the only important item on the résumé is this: "Been there. Done that."

If you've been on a mission trip, you're qualified to talk about how God works. If you've stood around a candle and prayed during the quiet hours of a church lock-in, you can talk about prayer. If you've ever been down and felt God pick you up, you can talk about grace. If you don't feel as though you've done any such thing…go…do.

Go to the other side of the lake.

Go on a mission trip.

Go feed those who are hungry and visit those who are sick.

Your life can be a message for someone else. Sharing the message of Jesus isn't about preaching and prophesying and saving. It's about one beggar showing another where the food is. Just be ready.

Once you get in the boat, there will be times when you must hang on for dear life.

When you say, "Yes, I think this is the path I want to follow," Jesus may turn your life upside down and send you on your way.

THE STORY CONTINUES

Go back to the picture you drew earlier. Draw Jesus on the boat. Ask him to calm your storms. Be very specific about what you want to happen. Let God know what's bothering you. Then be prepared to let go. Look for signs this week that God heard you.

THE MAN BORN BLIND

Based on John 9:1-41

Jesus and the Twelve were walking toward the city. It was hot and dry, and a great cloud of dust followed them. Just outside the city gate, they saw the usual crowd of beggars. (Beggars weren't welcome in the city, so they gathered outside the city gates.) Some were sick, some were disabled, some were simply unable to do anything else. So they gathered near the gate to ask travelers for money.

When Jesus saw the group, he got quiet. The others knew that when the rabbi got quiet, it usually meant something interesting was about to happen.

A man who was born blind held up his bowl. "Please?" he said.

Thomas, who'd been thinking deep religious thoughts all day, was eager to get some discussion going. He said, "Jesus, who was the bigger sinner—this man or his parents?"

Jesus gave him a puzzled look. "What?"

"He was born blind," Thomas explained, "so God must be angry. Is he being punished for something he did? Or is his blindness the result of his parents' sins?"

"Just some spare change, that's all," the blind man said.

Jesus looked first at Thomas and then at the other disciples, who were all glad Thomas had finally started the discussion. "Why do you need someone to blame?" Jesus asked.

"Okay, one coin," the blind man continued. "Any coin at all. Come on, man, I hear you jingling."

Jesus looked back at the man and then returned his gaze to the Twelve. Peter could tell by the look in Jesus' eyes that one of the Master's "teachable moments" had just opened itself up. "Watch this," Jesus said.

He took the blind man's hands and lifted him to his feet. "What? Did I do something wrong?" the blind man asked.

"Relax," Jesus said. The Son of God reached down and scooped up a handful of dirt. He spit into his hands several times and mixed the dirt and saliva with his finger. He then spread the resulting mud on the blind man's eyes.

The blind man said, "Hey, what are you doing?" He was surprised by the mud. He didn't see it coming because *he was blind!*

Jesus said, "Now go to the pool and wash the mud off your eyes."

The blind man wasn't impressed by this particular trick. He stumbled away mumbling, "Real funny, man. I bet you think you're hilarious."

The man navigated his way to the river. He felt the water on his toes and then his ankles. He bent low and, using his hands like a bowl, splashed water on his face. He rubbed the dirt from his skin and eyes before opening them.

"Hey...hey! I can see. I CAN SEE!"

The man stumbled and fell three times as he came out of the water. He'd never used his eyes to help him run or walk or even move before. "Hey!" he shouted.

He grabbed a nearby man by the front of his tunic and said, "Hey, I can see!" He let go and made a run for the city gate. He was soon laughing so hard that he could barely walk.

"Hey, I can see!!"

As he passed the city gate, laughing and shouting, people saw him and asked, "Isn't that the blind beggar from the city gate?"

Others said, "Nah, it just looks like him."

The no-longer-blind man ran headlong into a group of men who were haggling over the price of a large jar of olive oil. He nearly knocked them over. "I can see!" he screamed.

A man named Phillip who had much money (so people naturally assumed he was smarter than they were) grabbed the formerly blind man's face and looked into his eyes. The two men made direct eye contact. That's when the (until recently) blind man started to weep. He'd never made eye contact before.

He said it quietly this time: "I can see."

Philip, who was looking for a way to disbelieve, asked, "How?"

The (until just recently) blind man said, "There was a man named Jesus. He healed me."

One of the other men asked, "Who is Jesus? Point him out to us."

The (formerly) blind man shot him a look (which was a first for him) and said, "Like I'd know what he looks like. I was BLIND, for crying out loud."

Nothing like that had ever happened to these men before. So they did what people back in those days always did whenever something happened that had never happened before and required an explanation. They took the not-blind-anymore man to the Pharisees, who were considered to be the holiest and wisest of all men.

The Pharisees took turns looking into the eyes of the blind man who wasn't blind at all. Then they asked him, "How did you get your sight?"

The once-blind guy said, "It was Jesus. He healed me."

The Pharisees turned away and huddled together for a few minutes, arguing and mumbling as they often did. Finally they turned around and said, "Well, that settles it."

The nowhere-near blind man and the others who were present in the court looked at each other. "Settles what?"

The tallest of the Pharisees (at least the one with the tallest hat) said, "This Jesus obviously can't be the Messiah."

The man who now had two fully functioning eyes said, "He healed me."

The Pharisee said, "Yes, but he did it on the Sabbath. This is against the law. No Messiah would break one of God's most sacred laws." The other Pharisees folded their hands in front of their waists and looked up at the temple ceiling.

The gathered crowd gave a collective "Ohhhhhhhhhhhhhhhhhh," as if they understood.

But it was only the blind man who spoke up. He began dancing in circles, shouting, "I can see clearly now, the rain is gone!"

The Pharisees, who weren't used to being challenged, determined the man must be lying—he must have had his sight all along. So they sent word to have his parents brought to the temple.

The head Pharisee looked at the elderly couple as they clung to each other, and then he pointed to the ex-blind man. "There," he said. "Is *that* your son?"

Unsure about the proper answer, the elderly man said, "He looks like our boy, but it can't be him. Our son was born blind."

The not-at-all blind man recognized the elderly man's voice and called out, "Dad? Mom? It's me! I can see!"

The woman opened her arms and received her son into them. She grabbed his face, looked deep into his eyes, and knew for the first time that he was looking back.

The Pharisee asked, "How did your son get his sight?"

The elderly man said, "I wasn't there. Why don't you ask him?"

The man (who wasn't blind anymore) let go of his parents and turned to the Pharisee. "Look at me!" he said. "My eyes are working here. It's a miracle!"

The Pharisee crossed his robed arms and said, "Yeah, right. Come on, tell us what *really* happened."

The man whose eyes had recently been fixed replied, "I was blind. Now I see. What more do you need to know?"

The Pharisee who still wasn't considering even the *possibility* of a miracle, said, "Why don't you run through it just one more time so we can all understand?"

The man (who wasn't blind anymore) said, "Why? Do you want to follow him, too?"

(Author's Note: *Never* say that to a Pharisee.)

This question was immediately followed by a lot of shouting on the part of the Pharisees, not to mention some finger-pointing and several cries of "Sinnnn! Sinnnn! Sinnnn!"

The Pharisees roughly grabbed the not-even-close-to-blind man and hustled him through the streets. They shoved him through the city gate where he landed in a heap not too far from where he'd been sitting just a few hours earlier.

The Pharisees all turned around at the same time, brushed the dust from their long robes, and walked stoically back to the temple. "There," they said. "No harm, no foul."

The (until just recently) blind guy stood up and shouted at their disappearing backs, "Hey, idiots! Get your noses out of your scrolls. You're not going to find a dirt-and-water blindness cure anywhere in your rule books. Not even in the concordance!"

But they ignored him and walked back to the temple, where they could continue their discussion of when the Messiah might *really* show up.

The newly sighted man flopped down on the ground in disbelief. Then Jesus walked up to him and asked, "So how's that whole sight thing working out for you?"

The man stood up and asked, "Do you know who did this to me? Do you know who performed this miracle?"

Jesus spoke clearly, "Are you deaf now, too?"

The man cried, "Jesus!" and threw his arms around him, lifting the Master off the ground. The disciples stood back and watched, still trying to figure out what was going on and what they'd gotten themselves into.

When the man set Jesus down again, Jesus was laughing. He put his arm around the man who no longer had begging as his only career option and said to his disciples, "I do these miracles so those who are *figuratively* blind can see, too."

Thomas raised his hand and asked, "What does *figuratively* mean?"

As it turned out, not all of the Pharisees had gone back with the others. Some stood on top of the city wall and shouted, "What? Are you calling *us* blind?"

Jesus smiled at them and called up, "If you were really blind, then no one would blame you if you walked off a cliff. It wouldn't be your fault. As it is, you act like you can see everything from where you are. So when you eventually walk off the edge, you won't have anyone else to blame."

And still they didn't get it.

RANDOM THOUGHTS ABOUT THE STORY OF THE MAN BORN BLIND

Think about the board game or card game or sport that has the most difficult rules you've ever tried to learn. Cricket comes to mind, as does a card game called euchre. (I never could get that one. I'm also perfectly content with my *Lego Batman* video game. I tried playing *Left 4 Dead*, but it gave me a headache.)

Write down two game titles. One is a game you're so good at, you make it look easy. The other is a game you haven't mastered yet. Explain why you're so good at the first one.

Think about someone you know who's so into a particular game that he could quote the instructions from memory. If you envision that same type of person when it comes to the Bible, then you're picturing the Pharisees.

The Pharisees memorized the Old Testament. Every word. Even every space between the words. MEM-OR-IZED!

And they spent their days arguing about what each word *really* meant and what God *really* wants. Then they'd go out into the city and make sure everyone knew exactly how smart they were and how close they were to God because of their scriptural expertise.

It was all about rules for them. Even the disciples fell into that trap. The first thing they wanted to know was whose fault it was that this man was blind. Was God punishing him for something *he* did or something his parents did? (People often believed the sins of the father were visited on the son.)

Write down the one rule that you seem to have the most trouble with. It may be a school rule, a family rule, a sports rule, or a life rule.

Jesus tried to tell the Pharisees it's not about rules; it's about love.

And faith.

And believing.

But they didn't listen to him.

The Pharisees were so caught up in their rules that they couldn't see the miracle. *It's not a miracle if it happened on the Sabbath?!*

What's today's equivalent?

How do we stick our fingers in our ears and say to Jesus, "I can't hear you! La la la la la!"?

If your religion says, "God loves you...but..."

However...

Only if...

Except for...

Then how is that any different from what the Pharisees said? The miracle is right in front of us. Yet, too often we're the ones who ask, "What day is it?"

The people of Jesus' time believed that if you were healthy and rich, then God loved you. If you were sick and poor, then God was miffed at you.

Jesus came along and said, "God loves everyone."

He used the word *agape*. It means "loving without conditions or expectation of anything in return."

God loves.

That's it.

Pretty simple, really.

THE STORY CONTINUES

Draw a picture of a brick wall. On each brick write one obstacle that keeps us from accepting and loving others the way Jesus did. Then write down one way you can remove one of the bricks. Choose the easiest or hardest brick; it's up to you. How might removing that brick weaken the others?

DANIEL

Based on Daniel 6:1-18

Somewhere along the way, Daniel learned to enjoy praying. He wasn't sure when it happened. As a boy he could never stay focused long enough to pray—at least, not long enough to please his father. His father could pray endlessly.

Daniel would bow his head like his father did and squeeze his eyes shut tight to block out the distractions. But the sound of a bird or the rain or the funny noise people make when they blow their noses always grabbed his attention. Sometimes his father would simply tap Daniel's hand to bring his thoughts back to prayer. Other times his father would quietly reach over and gently thump Daniel's head with a finger. Either way, prayer was a struggle when Daniel was a boy. But now he looked forward to it.

On his knees…by his bed…inside his small room…up on the second story of the house—that's where Daniel liked to pray. Prayer was his lifeline. It calmed him. It renewed him. He said morning prayers for guidance. Afternoon prayers were for strength. And evening prayers focused on examination and introspection. When Daniel prayed, he felt connected to something bigger than himself. God was very real to him as he prayed.

Now Daniel prayed in his cell. He'd tried encouraging several other prisoners to pray with him, but they stood back and let him pray by himself. He wasn't worried, though some said he should be. He prayed in prison without even thinking about it.

Daniel's prayers had landed him in jail. What could they do if he prayed in his cell? Arrest him? He kneeled down and hugged himself. The cell was always cold in the morning. He'd expected to be taken to King Darius. Now he awaited Darius' decision.

Darius was a good man, but his mind was addled. In some ways he was still a child, while in other ways he was a wizened king. Daniel suspected that Darius would have been much happier if he could just go outside and play with his children.

Daniel had worked for Darius' predecessor, first in his kitchen and then as one of his administrators. The other administrators hated Daniel. They thought of him as some golden boy off the street with no training or experience. They even referred to him as "the king's new toy."

The fact that Daniel impressed Darius by doing such a good job only infuriated them more. The other members of Darius' council gathered to hatch a plan. The golden boy would have to go.

The administrators convinced Darius that because he was king, he must also be God—and therefore, his people should worship him. From there it was only logical to conclude that anyone who prayed to a god that wasn't Darius was disobeying the will of God (Darius) and had to be punished.

So King Darius, who liked the idea of being God (and who tended to believe the last person who told him things), signed a decree that all prayers should be directed to him. It was a written-in-stone order. A no-one-can-ever-break-this-law-for-any-reason-and-with-no-exceptions decree. Any prayer that wasn't directed to Darius was considered a crime against the king—and God—and was punishable by death.

Daniel finished praying and stood. When he turned around, he saw a prison guard had been waiting for him to finish. Daniel recognized him as one of the guards who'd pulled him from his room a few days earlier.

"How's your wife?" Daniel asked.

"Better," said the guard.

"I've been praying for her."

"Thank you," the guard replied. "The king would like to see you."

"Let's not keep him waiting," Daniel said.

Daniel knew the way to the throne room. He'd worked in the palace during most of his years in captivity. The guard was a huge man who often had to duck to get through doorways. Daniel could have bolted, disappeared in the maze of corridors, and eventually made his way outside. But he didn't.

They entered the throne room, and Daniel saw light coming in through the window behind the throne. The king certainly looked holy, with the sunlight shining down on him like that. Daniel had been in this room many times before. He'd advised the two Babylonian kings who ruled the region before Darius and Darius himself. Daniel wondered if this would be an advisory visit or a death sentence.

Three of the king's administrators stood off to the side clutching their scrolls, their evidence against him. They were ready for a fight.

"Daniel," King Darius said. He almost smiled. "True, then? You were praying to a god other than your king?"

"You are my king," Daniel said. "I ask my God to give you wisdom and long life."

"The king is God!" one scroll-clutching administrator shouted. "How can you ask the king to give himself long life?"

Daniel looked at the king and then at the administrator. "It's my God who gave me the wisdom to advise you well."

"He admits it, Your Majesty!" crowed the shortest of the accusatory trio. "He confesses to his crime of praying to a god and not Your Majesty. We have the law. It's a no-one-can-ever-break-this-law-for-any-reason-and-with-no-exceptions decree."

"I am the king," Darius said. "I will change the law."

"You are God," the small man reminded him. "You cannot break the law which God has put in place."

Darius gave Daniel a helpless look, as if the little man's words made sense. "Daniel," he said sadly, "may the god you worship spare you."

Daniel felt the guard's giant hand grip his shoulder and felt his stomach drop.

The lions were kept in a pit beneath the palace. They could be let out for the games and to be shown to visitors, but they were fed through a hole in the ground outside the palace. And when they were hungry, the lions could be heard throughout the palace.

When he served the king, Daniel had watched as the children of dignitaries crouched low and crawled up to the mouth of the hole. If they heard a roar, they'd scream and run back to their friends. Still, few of them had ever seen what a lion could do to a man. Daniel had seen. Daniel knew.

Now his stomach felt as deep as that pit as they led him away. There was no going back to the cell. The sentence had been passed. Daniel was led to the mouth of the hole. The guard he knew was on his left; another guard stood on his right. From the pit he smelled blood and dung and wet fur.

He turned to the two guards. "You don't have to do the—"

Before the words were out of his mouth, the guard he didn't know placed a massive hand on Daniel's chest and shoved. Daniel felt his feet slip off the edge of the pit. The light above him got smaller. He pictured himself landing on the back of a lion and immediately being disemboweled.

Daniel hit the ground hard. Too afraid to move, too afraid to say anything, he lay on his back and looked up at the two guards who were looking down at him. They were too far away for Daniel to see their faces. Were they angry? Upset? Was this just a job to them? As he lay there, the guards pushed a stone over the hole.

The darkness enveloped him. He couldn't see his hand in front of his face.

Daniel closed his eyes. There was no difference in the blackness that surrounded him. He rolled onto his stomach and cautiously rose to his knees and started to pray.

He wasn't aware of the light until he heard laughter. When he opened his eyes, he noticed the pit was getting brighter. He instinctively looked up but saw the stone hadn't been moved. This wasn't the yellow light of torches either. This was a blue, almost white light. Again, there was laughter. It startled him and he sat up.

Seven lions were lying along the wall. And lounging in the center of them was a man. He was easily twice, if not three times, the size of Daniel. His robe was white, and the light in the room seemed to be coming from him. His hair hung in long strands around his face. From where Daniel kneeled, he could see the creature's wings. Daniel stretched back onto his stomach and watched as a lion stood and put its two front paws on the angel's chest, pushing him back and pinning him to the ground.

"Oh, come on," the angel said, chuckling. "Now…now…let me up…come on."

The lion leaned in and licked the angel's face.

"That's enough now." The lion moved away, and the angel rolled onto his stomach and scrambled to his knees. He grabbed the lion's face in his two giant hands and said, "Who's a good kitty? Who is? Who is? Yes, he's a good wittle kitty." The lion lulled his head sideways and allowed the angel to scratch him behind the ears. He purred in a low rumble that Daniel could feel in his own stomach.

"Yeeeeesssss, he's a good wittle kitty, isn't he? Yes, he is. Yes, he is."

The angel sighed happily, as if he were truly enjoying the moment. He flopped backward and leaned against the body of another beast. Two other lions raised their heads to look at the angel and then at Daniel...then returned to their naps.

The angel looked at Daniel and laughed again. "If you could see the look on your face," he giggled.

The "good wittle kitty" pawed at the angel's hand. The angel once again stroked its fur and scratched the big cat behind the ears.

At dawn Daniel was awakened by a new light. He didn't remember falling asleep or seeing the angel leave. Yet he knew his head was resting comfortably in the soft hair of one lion's mane, while his feet were propped on the back of another.

As light from the surface seeped in, two lions grumbled and scooted out of the brightness. Daniel put a hand over his eyes and mumbled, "I know how you feel."

"Daniel!" a voice called from above. "Daniel, tell me you're still alive! Tell me that your God has saved you!"

It was the king.

"Who's the king?" Daniel called up without standing.

There was a long pause and finally Daniel heard the king's voice. It was both laughing and crying. "I am!" he called.

Daniel stood and stepped closer to the light. "Who's the king?!"

"I am!" the voice called again.

A rope was lowered into the pit. Daniel grabbed it and tugged twice. One of the lions looked up as Daniel was lifted to the surface. Daniel smiled. The lion stood and walked over to where Daniel had been standing.

Daniel smiled again as the king and one of his advisors pulled him through the hole. "Who's the king?!"

"I am!" the king shouted. "Who's alive?"

"I am!" Daniel shouted. The king embraced him as if he were a son who'd just come home after years of being away.

"I'm so glad you're not dead," the king said.

Daniel accepted the king's embrace and said, "My God sent an angel. You should have seen it."

Behind them the advisor—one of the ones with the scrolls, the ones who'd come up with the let's-eliminate-Daniel idea—said, "Your Majesty? There's still the matter of his crimes."

The king released Daniel and turned to the advisor. He motioned for the scroll, and the advisor came forward and handed it to him. "How about breakfast?" the king asked.

"I'd love to join Your Majesty for br—"

But before the advisor could finish, the king grabbed him by the front of his tunic, turned, and pushed him through the hole in the earth. Immediately from below came a loud roar.

Daniel thought, *Who's a good wittle kitty?*

RANDOM THOUGHTS ABOUT THE STORY OF DANIEL

Have you ever noticed that when people start playing God, they get into trouble? Does the phrase "God Himself couldn't sink this ship" ring any bells?

There was a time when people said humans weren't meant to fly. So much for that idea. What are some current ideas that make people say, "Humans weren't meant to do that"?

There have always been (and always will be) leaders who like to lead and leaders who like to be in charge. There's a difference. You probably already know this.

Like Jacob, back in the first chapter of this book, King Darius probably stayed awake all night thinking about his mistakes. Have you ever lost sleep over something you did? Do you think all good leaders second-guess themselves in private?

Sometimes we absolutely know the right thing to do, yet we follow the crowd simply because the right decision is just too hard to make. Where does this choice usually land us?

Draw a street sign of your own creation, one that symbolizes a sign you missed or ignored on your life journey.

Have you ever been so close to someone that it felt as though your ears missed him if you didn't hear his voice and your arms ached if you didn't hug him? Have you ever missed someone so much that you felt her absence physically, mentally, and spiritually? That's how Daniel felt when he was told he wasn't allowed to pray to God.

If you feel God's absence, remember that God didn't move—you did. No one has the right to get between you and God, to tell you there's only one way to worship or you can only "be" with God one way. That's not limiting you, it's limiting God. (And that happens to be impossible.)

The band Lost and Found has a song called "Lions." The chorus says, "Oh them lions they can eat my body, but they can't swallow my soul." Some have claimed that the rescue workers who sifted through the rubble of 9/11 were heard singing it.

What are your lions? List a few of them.

When it was all over, Darius issued a new decree. He basically said this…

There is only one God—count 'em, one.
God was, is, and will always be.
Everything is part of God's kingdom.
With God there is no zero.
God rescues.
God speaks.
And just to prove the point, God saved Daniel.

Pray openly. Pray without ceasing. Live your life as if it were a prayer. Pray with your heart. Pray without words. Open yourself to the possibility that you are completely and totally *heard*.

THE STORY CONTINUES

Using the letters of the word *one*, write down three ways you can show the world that God is part of your everyday life. Each response must start with "O," "N," or "E."

O

N

E

Live those words this week.

ELIJAH

Based on 1 Kings 18:16–19:18

Elijah stoked the fire with a stick. The smoke wasn't too bad, was it? Nah, he could live with that. And wood—there was plenty of wood, wasn't there? He didn't get a good look when he got to the cave, but he was sure there would be plenty—probably just beyond the mouth of the cave. And if there wasn't, he could get some at night, right? He could stock up. He never had to leave the cave again. He was safe. He was dry. He was warm.

Of course, there was the little matter of food. He'd have to hunt. He wasn't much of a hunter. He wasn't much of a fisherman either. But he could learn. There was no going back to the city, that's for sure. Not now. Not with Her Royal Highness in such a snit. Not after discrediting the queen in front of her subjects. Not after standing by and watching as an angry mob dismembered her priests.

What was there to be upset about? It was raining, wasn't it? As if in answer, the sky outside thundered quietly as the rain continued to fall. This was not a raging storm; this was a long, slow, soaking rain. This was the kind of rain that made farmers dance in their fields. The kind of rain that made children stay indoors and listen to their grandparents' stories about the great flood. This rain was a gift.

For three years the people had been without rain. Three years. Farms had died. Families were starving. Three years without rain, and every day Jezebel and a few hundred of her prophets made a big show of praying for rain and predicting that Baal would send down bucket loads. Three years and there hadn't been so much as a thimbleful of water.

You'd think Jezebel would be grateful for the rain. Politicians loved to take credit for the great and wondrous things that happened in their kingdom. Moreover, why didn't she see the truth? Why couldn't she tell that Baal—the god she was so fond of—was no more real than the stone statues she'd had carved? She'd been shown undeniable evidence that there was one God and that if you asked him nicely to make it rain, it would rain. But Her Highness didn't listen. She never listened.

Jezebel had instituted a government program to kill any and all prophets of God. Out of the hundreds that had been in the city, only one was left: Elijah. The contest had been Elijah's idea. One against 450. The odds didn't bother him at the time. But as he sat stoking the fire and listening to the rain, only then did it occur to him what a stupid move he'd made. He complimented himself on his faith. In truth, it never occurred to him to think otherwise.

He let the prophets of Baal go first. To build a fire. To sacrifice a bull. To pray for Baal to show himself. To ask him for rain. The prophets spent half a day dancing and chanting, cutting themselves and covering themselves in the blood of the bull.

Elijah sat on the sidelines. He thought of his opponents' display as an educational experience, a chance to learn a game when you have no idea what the rules are. But after so many hours, he just started to laugh.

"Sing louder!" he called. "Maybe Baal is in the bathroom! Are you going to keep this up all day? I've got things to do!"

When the last of Baal's prophets fell to the ground exhausted, Elijah stood. Everyone looked at him. Elijah looked at the sky, held out his hand, and then shook his head sadly at the prophets of Baal. By that time crowds were gathering. The contest of the gods had begun, and everyone wanted to watch.

Elijah built an altar using 12 large stones—one for each of the 12 tribes of Jacob (whose name God had changed to Israel). He dug a trench around the altar and then stacked wood on top of it. For his sacrifice, he butchered a bull and placed the pieces on the wood. Then he commanded that jars of water be poured over the pyre. For good measure, he instructed the trench around the altar to be filled with water, too.

By that time even the prophets of Baal were watching. People from all over the city waited to see what would happen. Elijah stood near the pile of soaking-wet wood and stone and looked up at the sky.

"God?" he said.

Immediately a ball of fire fell from the heavens and smashed into Elijah's soggy pyre. The wood, the bull, the stones—all of it—was incinerated in an instant. The water that filled the trench around the altar evaporated. When the smoke cleared, all that was left was scorched earth.

Elijah turned to the crowd that had gathered. "Get ready," he said. "It's going to rain."

But the crowd didn't leave. Instead they rushed forward, charging the 450 prophets of Baal. The prophets saw the mob coming and tried to run, but the crowd was on them like wild dogs. Elijah shouted, "Don't let them get away!"

Before long, the prophets of Baal had quite a bit in common with those butchered bulls. When the massacre was finished, the people, now covered in the blood of the prophets, walked back to their homes. They moved their giant water jars outside. They stood on the roofs of their homes, stretched out their bloodstained hands, and waited.

The rain outside the cave was starting to let up. It had rained hard for almost three days, drenching the fields and filling people's water jars. Some people stood outside and drenched themselves. Children who'd never seen rain or were too young to remember the last time it rained hid indoors while their fathers and mothers stood outside and danced in the downpour.

The only one who *wasn't* happy was Jezebel. She didn't care about the rain. She didn't care about the proof of God's superiority. She cared only about being shown up by one lowly prophet. She sent a message to Elijah: "When I find you, you'll wish you'd been treated as kindly as my prophets were treated."

That's why Elijah was now hiding in a cave where it was warm and safe and dry. All he needed was food. He hadn't eaten in three days.

Eventually he fell asleep. In his dreams he smelled sweet bread baking. When he opened his eyes again, he saw an angel of God. He thought God had sent the angel to take him to heaven. "Oh, sweet relief," he said. "I'm ready to be with God."

The angel laughed. She was beautiful. Her long hair hung down around her shoulders. Her robe was spotless. Her massive wings were folded behind her. She handed Elijah a plate piled high with sweet-smelling rings of dough, each one sticky with sugar and oil. "Eat," she said. "You'll need your strength."

Elijah devoured the bread within seconds. He was halfway through a second piece, licking the sugar from his fingers, when he suddenly looked up at the angel, worried. "Strength for what?" he asked.

"God wants to know what you're doing here. You have more to do."

Elijah felt his stomach drop. "I'm not going with you."

The angel smiled in a way that reminded him of his mother and shook her head.

"But they're trying to kill me," Elijah said.

The angel stood and began to tidy up the bowls and spoons she'd used to make the sweet bread. Elijah's eyes widened. Sitting by the fire, she'd seemed so much smaller, almost motherly. Seeing her stand before him now, in all of her enormity, he dropped his last bite of dough into his lap.

"Finish up," she said. "Then you're to go and stand at the mouth of the cave. God is going to pass by."

Elijah glanced toward the cave entrance. When he looked back, the angel was gone. He'd assumed the light in the cave was from the fire, but now he realized the fire was just glowing embers. The light had come from the angel's presence.

He ate the last bit of dough and stood. Wishing he had more but feeling fully satisfied in his belly, he stared at the mouth of the cave. If he just stayed where he was, maybe the angel would bring him more food. He doubted it. He took a deep breath and walked toward the cave's entrance.

Ducking low, he stepped out onto a small ledge and was nearly blown off his feet by a powerful wind. Forcing himself upright, he stood leaning into the wind, his robe blowing itself into tatters. His hair and beard were whipping in his eyes. Through the dust he could make out a funnel cloud. A hurricane. A great wind. He'd never seen one, but he'd heard stories of their destruction. The funnel cloud bounced around the canyon below.

Elijah watched until the wind spun itself out, its last tapers drifting away like smoke. He regained his footing on the ledge and suddenly felt a vibration beneath his sandals. The intensity increased until the whole mountain seemed to shake. Elijah steadied himself against the cave wall and watched as boulders the size of his home fell past him and shattered on the canyon floor. Elijah wondered if God was shaking his earth the way a child shakes a rattle. Smoke and dust blew up from below. Elijah put his hand over his face, partly to keep the dust out of his nose but mostly because he was scared of what might happen next.

He felt the fire before he saw it.

The heat of the flames made him step back—but not back into the cave. As a child he'd watched ants crawl near the flame that his mother cooked over and wondered what the fire must look like to them.

Now he knew.

The fire was a wall, like a sheet of fabric blowing on a clothesline. It flapped back and forth and wrapped around itself. The noise of the fire was deafening. The flame roared like an animal, screaming its presence and lapping at the canyon walls.

Then it died down as suddenly as it had appeared, and a single spark floated past Elijah's nose. He felt the smoke deep in his lungs.

Elijah stepped closer to the edge of the rock beneath his feet. A soft breeze blew past his face. It seemed to turn on its own and float past him from the other direction, gently blowing the dust from his hair and beard. The breeze encircled him. Elijah held out his arms and covered his face with his robe. The breeze blew through the folds of his robe. He laughed out loud. His fear melted into a sense of perfect safety. Never had he felt so comfortable standing before God.

The voice that whispered in his ear was full of love and assurance. It was compassionate, yet firm. It was welcoming, yet sending. It was understanding, yet instructive. It was a voice of pure love, and it spoke quietly in his ear.

"What are you doing here, Elijah?"

RANDOM THOUGHTS ABOUT THE STORY OF ELIJAH

I wish there was a way to know God's inflection. Did he ask, "What are you doing *here*, Elijah?" Or was it "What are you *doing* here, Elijah?" One seems to ask why he's in a cave, of all places. The other asks, "Why are you anywhere other than where I asked you to be?"

God whispers. God's voice is like a breeze. We might want a giant flashing neon arrow in the sky, but God is going to whisper and ask, "What are you doing here? This isn't where I want you to be. Go. Do what you're told. I'm going with you."

Draw four symbols of your own creation—one for "fire," one for "wind," one for "water" and one for "earth." Circle the one that best reflects the way God speaks to you—or the way you wish God *would* speak to you.

Elijah's faith was amazing during the contest with the priests of Baal. He confidently put on a great show. But when the soldiers came, Elijah ran and hid. How much of our own prayer is for show? How many of our "Christian actions" are done so people will know we believe? Why do we wear crosses like jewelry? What if everything that made us Christians had to be done in secret? What if Jesus had a facial tattoo and *that*, not the cross, became the accepted symbol of Christianity? How many of us would still be Christians?

There's a sense of urgency in Elijah's story. God seems to say, "What are you doing here *now*? You have things to do, people to see. So what are you doing here?" God sets things up so they'll happen according to his plan. Apparently, Elijah's flight wasn't part of that plan. Even so, God let him rest, gave him food and company, and then firmly—but not judgmentally—said, "Time to move on."

Self-pity dilutes whatever good you're doing. Don't let yourself start to think things like, *I'm the only one working on this mission trip. Everyone else is slacking off.* If you're there for God—really there for God—then the actions of others shouldn't enter into your thinking.

In Luke 9, Peter, James, and John went up a mountain with Jesus. There they saw the Lord bathed in a brilliant white light, talking with Moses and Elijah. In the Jewish faith, a place is set for Elijah during a Seder meal. When Jesus called out to God as he hung on the cross, people believed he was calling Elijah to come and save him. Elijah became an essential part of the Bible story. But in this passage, he's a scared man hiding in a cave.

At this moment you have no idea what God has in store for you. Even God says so. If you continue to follow God's plan, if you *choose* every day to try to serve him the best you can, you'll fit into God's plan the way the inner workings of a clock fit together perfectly.

In the space below, redesign the question mark. Create something that symbolizes life's decisions, something you could draw when someone asks, "What do you want to do with your life?"

Do what you're called to do.

Do it with faith.

Take a rest if you need to.
Then rise up and move on.

Above all else, listen to God's voice.

THE STORY CONTINUES
The modern equivalent of the "still small voice" might be a text message or "tweet." This week send the question, "What are you doing here, Elijah?" to a bunch of your friends electronically. When they get back to you to say, "Huh?" tell them the story.

EZEKIEL

Based on Ezekiel 37:1-28

Ezekiel was sitting at the head of the table. The elders of the tribe of Judah sat around him. They were all staring at him…waiting.

He'd grown to loathe these meetings. He was never a big fan of meetings anyway. Committees rarely made things better and usually made them worse, but this—this was hellish. The elders all sat around and waited for him to say something funny. The general consensus was that Ezekiel had gone off his nut.

Months ago he'd been in a meeting just like this one when suddenly a giant hand—yes, a *giant hand*—came into the room, grabbed him by his hair, and yanked him away. Everyone else in the room saw the giant hand. Everyone else saw him get yanked through the roof. But did the townsfolk say *they* were nuts? No. Just ol' off-his-nut Ezekiel.

The only difference, Ezekiel reminded himself, *was that the others had the good sense to keep their mouths shut.*

The hand of God had come into the room, lifted Ezekiel up by his hair, and shown him horrific visions. It was bad enough that God had asked him to walk around naked for years. Had he done that? Yes, he had. God also asked him to lie on one side for more than a year and then bake retched muffins and eat them in front of everyone. Had he done that? Yes, he had.

God described his people as two immoral sisters who did horrible, disgusting things. Had Ezekiel listened? Yes, he had.

Then God took Ezekiel's wife.

God warned, "I am going to take away the delight of your eyes." He told Ezekiel not to mourn—not to wear the clothes that mourners wear or eat the food that mourners eat. God said that would somehow get through to the people who'd missed every other message Ezekiel had delivered from God.

So far, though, the result was nothing. The people were as dumb as rocks. Ezekiel delivered his messages during the day; at night, while he lay alone and cold in his bed, he cried for all that he'd lost. He was just entertainment for the people. "Let's go to the council meeting and see what Ezekiel the nutball has to say today."

Ezekiel sat at the head of the table. He chaired the meeting. He followed all of the rules. And still they all looked at him as though they were waiting for the next crazy thing he might do.

"Are you even listening to me?" Ezekiel shouted. Suddenly their faces changed. Ezekiel knew immediately what they were looking at behind him. The hand was back. It grabbed him by the hair—the hair that had finally grown back after God told him to shave it all off. Once again Ezekiel was jerked out of his own home, carried high above the city, and dropped into an open field.

Ezekiel lay on the ground and coughed at the dust that wafted up from where he'd landed. He waved a hand in front of his face, and as the dust cleared, he found himself nose to nose with a human skull. Well, nose to nose *hole*, as it were.

"Ahhhhhh!" Ezekiel screamed. He scooted away from the skull and heard a crunching sound. Looking to his left, he saw that his hand rested on an armored breastplate surrounding a skeleton rib cage. A sword held the breastplate and what was left of the ribs in place, stuck fast in the ground. Ezekiel would later pride himself on not screaming a second time.

Jumping to his feet, Ezekiel felt bones break under his sandals. He leapt about, trying not to land on anything that was once human. That proved to be a challenge. When he finally found solid footing, he gingerly made his way across the valley. He looked around and saw no trees, no distant mountains, and no cities anywhere. Instead, he was tiptoeing where a great slaughter had taken place.

Thousands upon thousands of bones lay around him. Some of the skulls still wore helmets. Some of the hands still clutched the swords that pinned their bodies to the ground as though trying to release themselves. Ezekiel tried not to be sick. Unsuccessfully.

He looked up at the darkening sky and said, "Well?"

The voice of God came to him from all across the valley and from right next to his ear. It made the ground beneath his feet vibrate, while at the same time it sounded like it was just above him, the way his father's voice used to sound.

The voice said, "Ezekiel, are these bones alive?"

Ezekiel, assuming it was a trick question, replied, "Like I'd know."

God's voice became like thunder. "Preach to them."

"Preach to them?" Ezekiel repeated.

This time the voice came from right beside him. It was calm and quiet and utterly human. "Tell them that I am God. I will put them back together, and I will attach muscles to them. I will fill their veins with blood, and I will stretch fresh skin around them. They will stand up and know me."

Ezekiel looked around and hoped no one was watching him. Then he lifted his arms and said, "Hear me, bones!"

The bones didn't look like they were listening.

Ezekiel said, "Listen, bones. God is going to breathe across this valley. God is going to put you together. He's going to knit muscles onto you and sew veins into you and stretch fresh skin around you. You will stand up and know God."

The rattling sound that followed was almost sickening. It sounded like dry rain. Every shard of brittle bone that had broken away from the original moved across the ground and put itself back into place. Broken bones came together. The bones that had snapped beneath Ezekiel's feet now rolled away from him and reattached themselves to their original hosts. Toe bones became part of foot bones. Foot bones connected to anklebones. Anklebones connected to leg bones.

The skull that Ezekiel encountered when he was first dropped into the valley now stood on top of its skeleton. Its fleshless hands turned from gray to white and then reached up to straighten the helmet on his head. The skeleton was taller than Ezekiel, and it cocked its head to one side as if studying him with empty eye sockets.

One by one the skeleton army stood. The sound of metal clanging against bone grew louder. Ezekiel spun around and saw the vast army of bones now on its feet. All of the skeletal soldiers turned toward him. They stared at him with sightless eyes. One skeleton pulled a sword from its chest and then scratched at the empty space with a bony finger, as if the wound somehow itched.

The next sound was wet, as moist muscle and veins sewed themselves intricately through the bony framework of the soldiers all around him. Ezekiel could see blood coursing through the new veins. Lungs grew from nothing and attached themselves inside rib cages. Stomachs and organs filled with blood and fluid. The face that was staring into Ezekiel's suddenly grew two brown eyes that made the skull look more dead somehow.

As a boy Ezekiel had once watched with his friend Josiah as Josiah's dad, a tanner, stretched an animal's skin onto a wooden rack and began to clean it. It was a sound Ezekiel had never forgotten, and now he heard it again—times a million. Skin stretched over muscles, bones, and veins. It covered the faces and arms of the soldiers and turned them from a bleached white to something healthy and alive.

Finally, the man standing right in front of Ezekiel was whole. But Ezekiel could see deep into the man's eyes. There was nothing there. No soul. No sign of an inner being.

Ezekiel spun around again. The vast army of the dead surrounded him, staring at him with empty eyes.

Empty of breath.

Empty of soul.

The voice of God spoke to him again. This time it came like a whisper next to his ear. "Preach to them again. Tell them this: 'The four winds will come. They will pass through this place and breathe life back into you, and you will be whole again.'"

Ezekiel put his hand on the shoulder of the lifeless man in front of him. He said it quietly, knowing that if it were the word of God, then every ear would hear it. He said, "The four winds will come. They will pass through this place and breathe life back into you, and you will be whole again."

For the first time, the eyes of the man whose skull Ezekiel had nearly stepped on came into focus, as if they were connected to something besides an empty skull. A low hum echoed throughout the valley. Ezekiel looked around and realized the sound was coming from the men. Their voices were murmuring, calling, and eventually shouting.

"AhhhhhhhhhhhhhhhhhHHHHHHHHHHHHHHHHHHHHHHHHHHHHHHH!"

A massive chorus of pure noise rose into the air. Ezekiel covered his ears. The shouts soon began to reverberate, taking on different tones. Some voices began to sing. Others laughed out loud. The rejuvenated soldiers embraced one another as if they hadn't seen each other in years.

The voice of God spoke again. And Ezekiel realized he was the only one who could hear it above the din of laughter and song. "Ezekiel, are these bones alive?"

Ezekiel looked at the sky, caught up in the moment of life around him. "Yes, Lord."

God said, "These bones are like my precious children of Israel. They have dried up. They have no hope, no souls, no breath. I want you to go and preach to them. They will listen. Use my words and you will be heard. You will put life back into my people. I will give them a new place. I will put my life-spirit in them. I will make them whole."

Ezekiel stood looking at the sky. His joy faltered for just a moment. For that one moment, he was filled with questions.

How will they know?

How do I tell them?

What about those who still won't listen?

What if I mess it up?

What if…?

When…?

How…?

Then God's voice spoke to him clearly and answered all of his questions at once.

"Because I am God."

RANDOM THOUGHTS ABOUT THE STORY OF EZEKIEL

There are different ways to look at this passage. Do we take it literally? If so, we have to buy into the idea of a giant hand carrying Ezekiel by the hair. Or do we take it figuratively and view it as a very profound dream? Was it the Spirit of God who carried Ezekiel? Or was Ezekiel "in the spirit"—that is, was he having a vision? The image of the giant hand is too comical and the visual of a thousand skeletal bodies standing up like creatures in a zombie movie is too cool *not* to be taken literally, at least for our purposes here.

Any way you look at it, God was using this event to teach Ezekiel that the relationship between God and the people of Israel was going to get better. The valley, the dry bones, the bleached-out bodies—they all represented what God currently thought about the people he called his chosen ones.

We all have our own personal "valleys"—times or places in our lives that are so devoid of love and emotion that we feel like we don't even want to be alive.

Then God tells someone to preach.

It's been said that the difference between intelligence and wisdom is this: Intelligence means you learn things; wisdom means you understand that the lessons can come from anywhere.

What's the oddest lesson you've ever learned or the oddest messenger you've ever encountered?

You have your own personal Ezekiel. It might be a teacher or a counselor of some kind who simply says the right thing at the right time. Maybe today your Ezekiel is a song on the radio, a line from a book you're reading, a slogan on a billboard that for some odd reason strikes you differently today. In other words, someone says something that turns your day, your week, or your life around.

Think about a sermon, talk, or song that truly fed your soul. Sum up the message in one word.

We're talking about the breath of God—the Holy Spirit. You may know someone who seems to have it all together but is dry as dust on the inside. It's the breath of God that makes the bones alive. It's God's Word. It's God's Spirit that moves through a crowd and gives people back their voices.

Sometimes we're just going through the motions no matter how hard we try. When we connect with God, he becomes real and we become something more than ourselves.

God offers us a chance to collect ourselves. To stand again. We may be able to put our lives together, but God gives them meaning. God makes us real.

God breathes.

THE STORY CONTINUES

Think of the most holy word you've ever heard—a one- or two-word phrase that simply and succinctly sums up holiness for you. Got it? Now write that word on your palm using a permanent marker. Allow it to wear away naturally. Keep track of how many times you're reminded of the phrase over the next several days.

JOB

Based on Job 1:1–2:10; 38:1–42:6

Through his tears and through the rain, Job looked at his hands. What he saw were the hands of an old man. They weren't his hands. They couldn't be. His hands were strong. His hands had rings. His hands showed the signs of work and responsibility. His hands had carried and comforted 10 children. These were not his hands.

Job was kneeling at the tallest place he could climb to. The rain came so hard and in such tiny drops that each one felt as though it were cutting his skin. The wind had blown him against the rock several times. It had forced him to the ground. Job was finished. His body was still alive. His heart still pumped blood. His mind was still alert. But for all intents and purposes, he was dead. Spent. Job was empty.

How long had he been that way? He remembered the day it all started, but he couldn't remember when that was. It felt like a hundred years ago.

He remembered the sunshine. He remembered feeling the warmth of the sun on his face. He remembered the smell of fresh wood smoke on the sacred fires he'd built—fires of prayer—one for each of his 10 children. Every morning he built those fires himself and prayed, with his arms and eyes wide open, that God would protect his grown children, overlook their mistakes, and forgive their sins. And that particular morning the breeze had blown the smoke from his face, and Job knew God was a friend. He knew God would watch over him and his family. God would bless him even more than he had already. Job was a man at peace.

The servant's name was Julius, the son of one of the women who worked in the kitchen. Job had never liked him much. He was always whining about something. But Job would patiently listen to Julius complain about whatever issue was apparently ending Julius' world that day. Then he'd fix the problem or promise to have someone else fix it.

But right now Job was with God. It was his prayer time, his all-is-right-with-the-world moment. He treasured these times. Julius, on the other hand, brought nothing but trifles and annoyances.

"Master! Master!"

"Yes, Julius?" Job said with practiced patience. He didn't take his eyes off the sky.

"Master," Julius said more quietly. Job turned and saw his servant was covered in blood.

"Julius, what happened?"

Julius explained that the servants who'd been plowing the fields had been attacked. Men on horses had come and taken the oxen and the donkeys. They'd slaughtered the field hands. Only Julius had been left alive to tell his master what happened. With that, Julius pitched forward, fainting into his master's arms. Job caught him and gently lowered him to the ground. He patted Julius' cheek and offered him some water from the jar he kept nearby. But Julius was in a dead faint. Job heard the words again.

"Master! Master!"

Job turned. Another servant was running toward him. It wasn't a field hand. Job couldn't remember the boy's name, but he knew the lad worked with the sheep. "What is it?" Job asked.

"Master," the boy said, "I was coming back from the well with some water for your shepherds, when lightning struck the ground right in the middle of the field! All of your sheep are dead."

"All of them?" Job asked. He didn't remember how many sheep he had. Four thousand head? Five thousand? "Didn't the shepherds see the storm coming?"

"Your shepherds are dead, too," the boy reported.

Job, who'd been kneeling as he held the unconscious Julius in his arms, lost his balance and sat down hard on the ground. Julius' head landed in his lap. Job thought about his shepherds. How many of them were there? How many of their families were living on his property? The boys' words cut through his soul.

"Master, master!" Job didn't even speak. An older man servant who'd been with Job for years panted and fell to his knees at Job's side. He looked at the boy and the crumpled form of Julius while catching his breath. Then he said, "Master, your camels were stolen! The Chaldeans came and took all of them, plus all they were carrying, too. And the servants who cared for them were murdered as well."

Job had barely begun to register the loss of his field hands when he saw a woman, the servant of his eldest son, stumbling toward him. She was crying so hard she could barely keep her balance. Job asked the question, but his voice barely rose above a whisper. "What is it?"

The woman said, "Master, your children…they are…they were having a feast…and there was a storm…the house…the roof…master…they are all dead."

In the months that followed, Job came to look back on that day as the day he died. He didn't have time to grieve the loss of his servants and his property before learning he'd lost even more: All of his children. They were his life. Without them, Job wasn't really alive.

After that, Job moved through his days in a kind of fog. Finally, Job tore his garments—all of them. He shaved his head completely and went out to the front of his house. The servants who were left, the weeping families of the dead, and his own wife were waiting for him.

This is what Job said: "God gives. God takes away. Blessed be God's name."

Job's sadness overwhelmed him. He disappeared deep inside himself. When his friends came to his side, they sat in silence with him for seven days. At the end of the week, his friends concluded that God was punishing Job. And whatever Job had done had to be pretty serious because God had taken everything.

Job's friends told him that if he'd just confess his sin, God might let up. His wife said, "God hates you. How can you love a God like that? Denounce him. Let's get on with our lives." Job said nothing.

In time Job allowed the fog to clear. He allowed himself to feel again. All the pain, grief, and overwhelming sadness enveloped him. But Job's first feeling wasn't sadness; it was anger. He walked far across the land to a mountain and began to climb. Each step brought a darker sky. The wind nearly blew him over the edge. The rain soaked his torn clothing. It ran down his bald head and into his face. He spit out the rain rather than swallow it.

And when he finally came to a ledge large enough to stand on, he looked up at the thundering clouds and biting rain.

"Why?" he cried.

For the next few days, Job's anger and grief took over his very soul. He shook his fist at the lightning. He spit at the thunder. He demanded that God answer him. He pleaded with God to speak, to show himself, to give a sign. The lack of response just made Job angrier. The sky thundered and Job thundered back.

But he didn't curse God.

He didn't hate God.

He didn't justify himself before God.

He just wanted to know why.

Job fell to his knees in the rain. He covered his face with his old-man hands and looked through his fingers. He said, "Why? Why, why, why, why, why, why, why, why, why, why?" He repeated it until the word lost all meaning—just like his life. Job was finished. He was empty.

"Stand up and face me," God commanded.

Job stood and looked at the sky. The black clouds parted just enough to let a light of unimaginable brightness shine through. Job started to hold up his hand to shield his eyes but changed his mind. He planted his hands at his sides and looked into the light.

God said...

"You want me to answer your questions? I made the universe. What have you done?

"Tell me about the earth, Job. How fast does it spin? Where is the lightning kept? How were the oceans dug out? Huh? Do you know? Who made the clouds? Tell me what song the stars were singing while I set the cornerstone of this rock you call home in its place. Do you have an answer for me?

"Did you order the sun to rise? Did you create the phases of the moon? Tell me what wonders lie in the caves at the bottom of the ocean. Do you know what *was* before there was anything? Do you know what comes next? You have your ideas, but do you truly know? What makes rain? What makes hail? Where do I store the thunder when I'm not using it?

"Do you know the first thing about the stars? Do you still believe they're just pinholes in my black robe? Can you make Orion hunt for you? Can you make the great bear growl?

"When does the deer give birth to her young? Have you seen it happen? Have you seen any of my animals raise their young, protect their caves, kill their enemies? Were you even aware this was going on?

"Who let the wild ass go free? You can bring the animals in from the world. You can take them and subject them to your control, but can you free them? Can you put in them the desire to run, to climb, to soar? Do you honestly believe that if you hitched your plow to a buffalo, it would do as you commanded? Do you think it wouldn't kick and take your head off?

"Tell me about horses. Did you design them? Can you hear what they think? Do you know why they don't run away from battle? Do you know why they seem to sense what's coming and run forward anyway?

"Have you filled the ocean with creatures beyond your comprehension? Can you imagine what's beyond your imagination? Creatures live in my oceans that would swallow you if you got close enough to touch them. You have no idea."

Job replied, "I...uh..."

"Have a seat," God continued. "Now answer me this. You think you know better than I do? You think you can look into a man's heart and say whether he's a sinner or a saint? Can you make your voice sound like thunder? Could you wipe the wicked off this planet? Could you dig a massive grave and kill all of the people you deem unworthy? Could you let a child die if it meant a thousand more would live?

"Can you do that, Job? Do you want my job?

"Do you know any of this? And now—now you think that because you've suffered loss I'm responsible to *you*? That I should bow to your command? You think you can sue me?"

Job felt his skin vibrate as God's voice passed over him. He knew the voice could shatter a forest. He knew God's hands could play with the sun like his children once played with a ball. Job was suddenly overwhelmed by the enormity of God.

He was aware of a great depth all around him:
A height
A breadth
An expansion of presence that wrapped around him
Becoming closer than his own skin.
At the same time, it was distant like the moon
Beyond the moon
Beyond the stars
Beyond *beyond*.

In this moment of pure clarity, there was no time. No beginning. No end. There was only *now*—an eternal *now*. Job felt like he was both falling and soaring...being filled and being emptied...being pulled apart and being crushed. It was a joy that radiated through his body and out the ends of the hairs on his head. It was a sorrow that broke his heart into pieces smaller than grains of sand.

Eventually Job became aware of the water dripping from his soggy hair and into the palms of his hands. He became aware of his robe clinging to his skin. He became aware of the light around him and realized he'd been in the dark. He became aware of the ground under his knees. His awareness rose like the dawn.

"I'm sorry," Job said. "Forgive me."

RANDOM THOUGHTS ABOUT THE STORY OF JOB

You can pray in church with your hands folded in front of you. You can pray while holding hands and standing in a circle around a candle on the last day of a mission trip. You can pray on your knees in a filthy parking lot in the pouring rain.

What is your favorite prayer position? What is your favorite prayer location? Draw a picture of it.

If you've ever done the limbo, you're probably familiar with the song, "Limbo Rock," which asks the frightening question, "How low can you go?" What if you had to find out? What if you woke up to the worst day of your life…and it slowly got worse? We've all had those days where we can say, "Well, at least I have _____." But what if you didn't? What if even *that* was taken from you?

Job was a good and faithful servant when he had everything. And he was *still* a good and faithful servant after he *lost* everything. He was just very angry.

Anger toward God isn't new. Read the Bible. It's full of people who scream at God. Anger toward God isn't wrong either. Disbelief, apathy, ignorance—*those* are problems.

Even if you're angry with God, you still believe. There's still a relationship there.

That's where many atheists get it wrong. They believe that because there's unhappiness in the world, God must not exist. But God doesn't cause unhappiness. Unhappiness happens. That's why God gave us each other.

I'll repeat that, just in case you're skimming this part: God doesn't cause unhappiness. Unhappiness happens. That's why God gave us each other.

Create a bumper sticker that communicates that truth.

Why do we fail to think about God when things are going well? We can have the best day we've had in months, and it never crosses our minds to say, "Thank you." But when the rug is pulled out from under us, *then* we start to pray: "Help me, God!" Or worse yet: "Why are you doing this to me?"

We become like that student who decides she's failing a class because the professor hates her. She didn't study much. She didn't show up for class regularly. She didn't ask for help when she needed it. She never participated in class discussions. But according to her, she's failing because the professor hates her.

God's ways are beyond our understanding. Job says: *God gives. God takes away. Blessed be God's name.* How hard would it be for you to say that—and mean it?

God knew what he was going to give to Job in the end. It's like someone holding the keys to a BMW behind his back while asking you for your skateboard. And it's not a trade—the person just wants to take your skateboard. The BMW will come later.

THE STORY CONTINUES

In this story God let Job rant. He listened and listened until Job fell breathless and exhausted. Then God said, "It's my turn now. Sit down, Sparky, and listen."

"I am God.
You are not.
There's a reason for that."

We all need that reminder every once in a while.

Come up with a simple tune to go with the three lines above: "I am God. You are not. There's a reason for that." Sing it to yourself throughout the week as a reminder of who's in charge of your life.

MARY MAGDALENE

Based on John 20:1-18

Mary of Magdala braced herself against the entrance to the tomb and wept into her hands. She could smell the myrrh from when she dropped the jar a few hours earlier. His body was gone. The stone was rolled away and Jesus was gone. Could they take anything else from her? They took his life. They told her she couldn't prepare his body for burial because it was the Sabbath. Now they'd even taken his body. "Why can't they just leave us alone?" She choked on her tears and fell to her knees, burying her face in the soft grass.

This wasn't even his tomb. They'd borrowed Joseph's family crypt. And Joseph, the lawyer from Arimathea, had risked his social standing by asking Pilate for the body. Pilate agreed but then ordered that the stone and two Roman guards be placed there as well. Now the stone was moved, the guards were gone, and the tomb was empty. It was an emptiness Mary felt deep in her soul. She *was* this tomb. Jesus was gone and she was empty.

Jesus had once told her that Joseph of Arimathea reminded him of his own father—his own Joseph. Mary hadn't met Jesus' father, but she knew his mother. After that she'd casually studied the Arimathean to get a small hint of what Jesus' father was like. Of course, Jesus had a way of looking into a person's heart. So the resemblance to his father may have had nothing to do with the way Joseph looked.

The butchers took Jesus. They nailed him to that horrible cross.

They killed him. They let him bleed, let him suffer. When it was over, his mother had cried on Mary's shoulder. She'd cried so hard that Mary had to hold her up. Eventually, though, they were both kneeling in the rain. Mary remembered looking at the puddle of blood—his blood—beneath the cross and noticing how the rain splashed in it, diluted it, washed it into the dirty ground. His mother cried and cried and cried.

The light started from inside the dark tomb.

Mary knew what angels were. She'd once overheard her father tell a neighbor about the night a group of shepherds claimed they saw a choir of angels in the sky over Bethlehem. The men agreed that a great deal of wine must have been involved, but Mary was always curious about the story. One day while she was sitting at breakfast with Jesus' mother, his mom told Mary the story of the angel who'd told her about the miracle that would take place. And Mary's older brothers often told her stories from the Torah about angels—warriors of God who wielded gigantic swords and wore glowing armor.

Inside the tomb stood two figures, one man and one woman, but they appeared somewhat blurry. Mary wiped the tears from her eyes to clear her vision, but the figures didn't come into focus. They weren't warriors or singers. They weren't giants. How could they be angels?

Mary could see their features. She could see their wings and the bright lights that surrounded them. The scent that wafted out of the tomb wasn't that of a crypt—damp, stale, death—but of sweet baking loaves...of clean fresh linens...of the ocean...of summer grass...of evening rain.

"Why are you crying?" the female figure asked Mary. It was a voice unlike any she'd ever heard. The figure didn't ask this question in sympathy but in disbelief. She was almost chuckling at Mary, just like Mary's mother used to do when Mary was being silly.

Mary rose up on her knees and said, "Please, they've taken him from me. If you know where he is, tell me so I can prepare the body."

Both figures started to laugh. Together they said, "He's not here."

It was too much for Mary. She buried her face in her hands once again and bent over with an ache so deep that she felt as though her heart would shatter like the jar of perfume she'd dropped on the rocks. She could hear herself breaking inside.

The light inside the tomb dimmed and went out. Then a voice from behind her asked, "Why are you crying?" It was a real voice this time—full of sympathy.

Mary thought it was the gardener. "Please," she said in a pleading tone, "if you've taken him... if you saw...if you know where he...his body is...please...please won't you tell me?"

"Mary," Jesus said, just the way he used to. She turned and saw him standing there. He was smiling.

Mary jumped up and threw herself into his arms, clutching him and burying her face in the folds of his robe. "Ah...ah," was all she could manage.

Wide-eyed and weeping tears of joy instead of sorrow, she started to laugh. She yanked her face away and looked up at him, then pulled him close to her again.

"Cmwifmie," she said into his robe.

Jesus laughed and stroked her hair. "What?"

She pulled her face away and said in a rush, "Come with me. We have to...no, first we...we have to go see Peter.... He's at John's house and...you have to go see your mother.... No, you have to hide.... They'll be looking for you."

Jesus said, "Shhhhhhhhh, you can't hang on to me like that. It's all different now."

"What are you talking about?" she asked. "You're alive!"

He laughed again. "I know."

She started to laugh, too. He said, "It's all different. You and the others, you'll have to keep things going by yourselves."

She looked at him and then held him close, tighter this time. She was terrified to lose him all over again.

Jesus pried her hands loose and gently touched her cheek. "I'm going to be with my Father," he said. "It can't ever be like it was. You can't cling to the past."

"No!" she said. "You can't go."

He smiled. "I'll be with you forever. But right now I need you to go into the city and tell Peter and John that I'm alive and I'm coming to see them."

She grasped his hand between hers, too scared to let him go.

"It's going to be okay," he said. "Go and tell them. I'm going to be with my Father, and their Father, and your father—with my God, and their God, and your God."

She smiled. He was definitely back. And already he was talking about things she couldn't comprehend. Gently, as if she were releasing a butterfly, she let go of his hand and turned to walk out of the garden. But by the time she reached the road, she was in a full-blown run. Her joy carried her as if she had wings.

She knew John's house. She knew Peter and some of the others would be meeting there. When she arrived, she hit the door so hard that she broke the wooden latch on the other side. Peter, who'd just been imagining what he'd do if Roman soldiers burst in and tried to take them away, fell over backward in his chair.

"He's alive!" Mary said.

Peter sat up and shook his head, rubbing the back of it with his hand. "What?"

John entered the room from the back of the house. "What?"

Mary twirled in place like a leaf on the breeze.

"She's lost it," Peter said. John nodded.

Then Mary grabbed Peter by the front of his tunic and yanked him to his feet.

Looking directly into his eyes, she said, "HE...IS...ALIVE!"

RANDOM THOUGHTS ABOUT THE STORY OF MARY MAGDALENE

Mary got it. When the other disciples were standing around saying, "Uh...Jesus? Could you go over that again?" Mary got it. Every time we meet her in Scripture, it seems she's acting out of gratitude and appreciation. She understood.

Mary was probably a woman of wealth who helped fund Jesus' ministry. We know she traveled with a group of men at a time when it was highly uncommon for women to do so. It would seem there was very little about Mary that *wasn't* highly uncommon.

Mary was one of three people who stayed with Jesus through his crucifixion. The disciples ran and hid. Maybe they watched from a distance; we can't be sure. But Mary was close enough to hear Jesus' gasps...and his last words. Mary stayed with him.

Draw a simple sketch of three crosses on a hill. Draw a stick figure to represent you. Where do you stand in your relationship to Christ? (Be honest. There's nothing wrong with having questions and doubts.) Are you close enough to hear the wheezing in Jesus' lungs or are you watching it all from a safe distance? Write down a word that represents a time when you felt closer to Jesus than you ever have.

Mary had an uncomplicated faith. The disciples argued over who was the greatest and who knew the most Scripture. Mary simply believed.

Imagine that you're getting a tattoo of one word that sums up your beliefs. The tattoo won't be on public display—nothing fancy, just one word. Write the word.

Jesus' greeting outside the tomb is perhaps the most wonderful one-word sentence ever: "Mary." It's the word that birthed an entire religion. Think about that. Everything we are as Christians today began with the word "Mary."

The stone wasn't rolled away so Jesus could come out of the tomb. He didn't need to have it moved. The stone was rolled away so Mary and the other women could go in. At a time when women weren't treated as equals, Mary's rabbi let her in. At a time when Jesus could have appeared to the disciples first, Mary was let in.

Mary was something of an enigma. Some scholars believe she was a prostitute at one time; others believe she was Lazarus and Martha's sister. The name *Mary* shows up in a number of different places, but we have no confirmation that any of them were the same Mary. The one consistency among all the Gospels is that Mary was let in. She was there at the foot of the cross, and she was there at the tomb—the first person to see the resurrected Christ.

Some versions of the resurrection story portray Jesus as some sort of translucent spirit. They suggest that Mary would have passed through him if she tried to hug him and that's why Jesus said, "Do not cling to me." But later he offered his nail-scarred hands and pierced side for Thomas to see and touch.

When Jesus said "cling" or "cleave," he used the word *dabak*, which means "to stick" or "to be glued to." The question isn't whether Mary did or didn't cling to him. The question is, "Wouldn't you?" After all they'd been through together, Jesus would've had to pry her loose and Mary would've rather done anything than let go of him—again.

Jesus comes into our lives, and very often he seems to wreck everything. Most of us like the lives we have. But when Jesus shows up, everything gets turned upside down. Quick case in point: I was going to be a radio DJ—that was my major in college. Then I had a daughter and a son and a job teaching teenagers about Jesus. Now I'm nowhere close to where I thought I'd be. Jesus "wrecked" me.

Mary had her own life as well. The disciples were fishermen and tax collectors. They also had their own lives. Then Jesus showed up and changed everything. He sent them into the world with a simple word: "Go."

Now it's up to us. We have to take the message to others. We have to show unconditional love. Then, when we feel most alone, Jesus shows up—as a kind word, a surprise gift, an encouraging email—and we're filled once again and ready to keep moving.

Every time Jesus shows up, nothing stays the same.

THE STORY CONTINUES

Now it's up to us. We have to take the message to others. We have to show unconditional love. Then, when we feel alone, Jesus shows us a kind word, a surprise gift, an encouraging email and we're filled once again and ready to keep moving.

Every time Jesus shows up, nothing stays the same. This week, be the Jesus that "shows up." Send a letter or an email. Give a compliment to a stranger. Hold a door for someone. You don't have to hold the door and say, "Jesus loves you." Just hold the door. Be the message. Write down your thoughts as you try to live out the "love everyone" life.

SAUL/PAUL

Based on Acts 9:1-22

As Saul rode he listened to the clang and jangle of the shackles that hung from the wagon behind him. The sound reminded him of the chimes hanging in front of his grandmother's fabric booth in the marketplace. He often played there as a child, and he used to listen to the chimes from his spot under the table (when he was supposed to be taking a nap).

But these clanging sounds weren't chimes. They were chains—black, ugly, forged instruments of imprisonment. They jangled as they dragged along the stone streets. And they were usually accompanied by the sounds of moaning and weeping from the people they imprisoned.

Saul often thought of those sounds as music, though he never said it out loud. To say he enjoyed the sound of women crying and men cursing him—to admit to enjoying that—seemed wrong somehow. But Saul *did* like it. He dreamed of it. He often hummed old songs as he listened to the chains. He was good at his job.

Neither of the two men who accompanied him on this trip was good at it. They had too much sympathy. Oh, they pretended to be like him—to be cruel and to act justified in their cruelty. But Saul knew they sometimes loosened the chains of the women and children. They showed mercy. Saul would have them both arrested when they returned to Jerusalem. There was no room for mercy in this job. Those people in chains were radicals. They defied God. They *mocked* God. And God had given *him* the task of rounding them up and hiding them away so this new faith—the "Way"—wouldn't get out of hand.

Saul never met the radical rabbi these people followed. The Romans had crucified the man called Jesus years earlier. Then, according to Saul's grandfather, Jesus' followers had stolen his body and run through the streets claiming he'd risen from the dead. They were defilers of the dead, Saul's grandfather had said.

When he was a boy, Saul had watched as one of Jesus' followers was stoned to death in the marketplace. Saul's grandfather was holding his hand as they walked among the tables full of goods. A woman gave Saul a fig to snack on. Then they walked outside the city a little ways and came upon an angry crowd of men. They were shouting as a man standing on several bales of hay preached to them. The man was pleading with them to listen—pleading with them to hear the words of the rabbi.

Saul's grandfather let go of Saul's hand, picked up a rock, and threw it at the street preacher with all his might. The throw went wide and missed the preacher's head by a foot. "Curse this infernal cloak," his grandfather muttered.

Saul's grandmother had made the cloak, and Saul's grandfather hated it. It was too bulky and warm for a man who seemed hot and angry most of the time. He took off the cloak and said, "Hold this, boy." Saul held out his arms and his grandfather laid his coat in them.

Within minutes, other men had laid their cloaks in Saul's arms as well. Then they picked up their own rocks and hurled them. The preacher's face was bloody and broken. He cried out to his God, but apparently his God ignored him because the man was soon crumpled and lifeless.

The men came back and took their cloaks. Some of them patted Saul on the head for being a good little man. His grandfather was breathing heavily as he wrapped his cloak around himself.

Saul said, "Grandpa, that man was calling to his God. Is his God the same as our God?"

Saul's grandfather drew back to strike the boy but then didn't. Instead, he knelt on one knee and said, "Listen to me, boy. These men—these preachers who follow this new religion—are deluding themselves. They're trying to tell us that Messiah has come and gone. If Messiah had really come, then we'd all be in paradise. The city would be ours. The Law says we cannot allow men to follow the wrong God. And those who try to lead men astray are abominations. God hates them. What you saw today was necessary. It's what God wanted."

Saul snapped out of his reminiscence when he heard Malachi riding up behind him. Malachi was Saul's age, and Saul liked him, for the most part. But Malachi was in this for the money. He took the coins Saul gave him at the end of a run and went into the city to find wine and women. Saul liked the money, too, but he was doing this because it was God's work. Someone had to do it, and Saul was good at it.

"Don't you think the chains are too loud?" Malachi asked. "We may as well send a messenger to the center of Damascus to let everyone know we're coming."

Saul stared straight ahead. "Good," he replied. "We want them to know we're coming. We want them to know we'll take their men and women. We want them to be afraid."

Malachi waited for more. Saul finally looked over at him and sighed. "If they're afraid, they hide. And they usually hide together. It makes them easier to find."

Malachi smiled. Saul glanced at his filthy teeth and turned away.

"More prisoners, more money," Malachi said.

There it was, Saul thought, *the simplest terms*. Maybe he wouldn't have Malachi arrested after all. But he was still planning to get rid of the boy. Amalek was only 15 and he was weak. He'd listen to the cries of the women and have pity on them. There was no room for weakness in this job. This would definitely be Amalek's last trip.

Saul looked down at his robe and saw a stain. Most likely blood. It was probably the blood of the old man from the last trip. He'd fallen again and again until his knees and feet were bloody. Saul had climbed down from his horse, lifted the old man to his feet, and spit in his face. He'd warned the old man, hadn't he? He'd warned him several times that if he couldn't keep up, he'd be executed right there on the street and his body would be left for the wolves. The old man pleaded and continued walking, his feet and wrists raw and bloody. When he fell again, Saul ordered Malachi to kill him. Malachi didn't think twice about of the loss of bounty. He was in a hurry to get to the city anyway, so it was no loss to him. Saul turned and looked at the old man who knew he was going to die. A woman screamed at Malachi to stop. She was probably the old man's daughter. Then the old man looked right at Saul and said, "I forgive you."

All these days later, his statement still bothered Saul. It was the same thing the street preacher had said to the mob as they threw stones at his head: "I forgive you." Who would say that? Was that part of the "Way"—to be stupid enough to forgive the people who kill you? That was just wrong.

Saul thought about the old man and the blood spot on his robe, about his grandfather, and about the scraping sound of the shackles as he rode along.

That's when the sun suddenly got brighter...and then went completely dark. At least, that's the way it seemed to Saul. He raised his hand to shield his eyes from the glare, but it was too late.

The darkness came instantaneously. He felt something covering his eyes. Saul jerked his head back and reached up to his face to brush away whatever it was. But in that moment he felt two large, rough hands on either side of his chest. (In later years as he thought back on it, he tried to imagine them as anything other than hands. But it wasn't possible.)

Suddenly the hands shoved him hard, and he rolled over backward right off his horse. He braced himself for an impact with the ground, but it didn't come. Instead, he was upright—standing on his feet. But there was nothing beneath him. Disoriented, he spun around and fell to his hands and knees. But again, he felt no ground beneath him.

"Malachi!" he yelled. No answer. There was no sound at all. He was in complete darkness and complete silence.

Then the wailing started.

A thousand voices at once. All of them in unison. All of them screaming his name: "Saaaaaaaaaaaa-aaaaaaaaaaaaaaauuul!"

The sound was deafening. Saul put his hands over his ears, but it didn't begin to blot out the noise. The wailing grew louder in his head. "Saaaaaaaul! Saaaaauul! Saaaaaullllllllllll!"

Saul screamed, "Who are you?"

The darkness covered him. It enveloped his entire being. He could feel the darkness in the strands of his hair and in the tips of his fingers. It was cold. The emptiness was tangible. Saul had never felt so alone—or so deeply lost.

"Saaaauuuul! Saaauuuul! Sauuul! Saaaauuuul! Saaaaauuuuuul!"

"Who are you?" Saul screamed again.

A wave of warmth washed over him, as though he were kneeling in the surf. But there was no water. The wave was a feeling of pure love and peace and relief. It subsided like an ocean tide and rolled back into some unknown sea.

"Who are you?" Saul barely spoke the words this time.

The next wave of warmth knocked him down. Had he been in the water, he would have come up spitting salt and seaweed. But he was dry. He clambered to his knees again and felt a hand on his shoulder. The hand steadied him.

Then a voice said, "I am Jesus. Why are you persecuting me?"

Saul began to shake with fear. He buried his face in his hands. He wept. Once again he felt the hand in the middle of his back. The touch was gentle. It reminded Saul of the way his grandmother used to wake him from his nap as a child. The hand radiated a peace that Saul had never known. His anger, his hatred, his ignorance, his confusion, his stress, his tension—all of it was lifted out of him. Saul felt as though he was being ripped open. He'd never known such a feeling. In his whole life, he'd never known such peace.

Saul blinked his eyes and sat up. He was still in the dark, but he was no longer afraid of it. He opened his arms, resting the back of his hands on his knees. He said, "My God, what would you have me do?"

The hand that belonged to Jesus touched his face almost tenderly. "Go into the city," the voice said. "You'll be told what to do."

The warmth, peace, and love that had washed over him rolled back into the unseen ocean. Saul became aware of the rocks in the road beneath his knees. He smelled the air around him. He heard the voices of his companions calling his name from some distant place. But their voices continued to get closer and louder until they were right beside him, yelling in his ear. Saul's eyesight didn't return.

"Saul!" It was Malachi. Saul turned in the direction of his voice.

"Malachi?"

Malachi seemed to breathe a sigh of relief. "What's going on? What happened? What's that stuff on your eyes?"

Saul put his hands to his face. His eyes weren't just closed; they were covered with some sort of scales, like the skin of a fish. Saul was shocked, but he wasn't afraid.

He turned his face back toward Malachi. "Take me to the city," he said.

His companions helped Saul to his feet and led him to Damascus.

RANDOM THOUGHTS ABOUT THE STORY OF SAUL/PAUL

This is the man who wrote the majority of the New Testament. This is the man who put Christians in prison, who held men's cloaks while Stephen was stoned to death. This is the man who wrote (in 1 Corinthians 13), "Love is patient. Love is kind."

Who is the most hated person in the country right now? (Don't write the name of a teacher you don't like. Most people don't know them.) The most hated, reviled, despised person in the country right now is:

What would you do if that person said, "Jesus spoke to me. I have a message"?

Later, when Saul was going by the name Paul, he wrote a letter to the people of Philippi (picture Vegas without the light show). He wrote to them while he was in prison, probably chained to a wall. Yet in that short letter, he used the word joy more times than any other book in the Bible.

Take a few minutes to load up this page with happy words—Joy, Dancing, Laughter or any other words you can think of. Fill the page. What if that were your life? What if there was so much happiness in your life you could not fit it all in? How would that change your outlook on the world?

Do you think God can't use you? Do you think you're such a nobody or such a bad person that God could never do anything remarkable with your life? Think again.

Other than Jesus, probably no other person shaped Christianity as much as Paul did. Read his stories in the book of Acts. He escapes from prison, survives a shipwreck, and does a nifty trick after he's bitten by a poisonous snake. Paul was the Bible's action figure. (Picture Will Smith starring in the movie version of his life.) And Paul led a mission team that took the message of Jesus across the Roman Empire.

Paul wasn't without his flaws. He was human, not perfect. But his intensity for God never waned. For Paul the message was full contact. He was an in-your-face kind of preacher; but it was always about the message, not about him.

Apparently, Paul was a long-winded preacher. There's a story in Acts 20 that describes how a teenager, named Eutychus, fell asleep during one of Paul's sermons, tumbled out of a three-story window, and died. Paul went downstairs, threw himself on the guy, and brought him back to life.

Just for fun: Have you ever fallen asleep during a sermon? If you have, write a bunch of Zs at the bottom of the page.

God doesn't waste your time. He'll use all of you—your past, your present, and your future—if you're willing to give them over to him.

You'll never know all of the wonderful and amazing things God can accomplish through you until you're willing to give him all that you are.

THE STORY CONTINUES

Draw a box. Imagine the box is going to hold the best part about you that you can give to God—your singing skills, your artistic ability, your ease with kids, your listening skills, your intelligence or anything else you can think of. Draw a symbol to represent it in the box. (Don't take up the whole box. Leave some room.) Now draw a symbol for the worst part of you—the part that you wish you could just forget about. (You don't have to share this part.) With your pen or some markers, "wrap" the box and put a bow on it. Remind yourself that God is going to use it for his purposes.

CORNELIUS AND PETER

Based on Acts 10:1-36

Cornelius was a big man. In his entire life, he'd never been considered small or frail or weak. Even as a toddler he'd been bigger than some of his older siblings. When he was 12 and learning the Torah, he could look the rabbi in the eyes. By age 15 he was towering over his father, his arms had grown to a massive size, and he had to duck through doorways.

To no one's surprise, Cornelius was recruited into the Roman army as soon as he was old enough to enlist. And it wasn't long before he was promoted to captain. Eventually, Cornelius got himself a house and a family. He had a pretty wife who was a great deal smaller than he was, and he enjoyed picking her up unexpectedly. She'd always slap at him playfully before she embraced him, and then he'd gently set her down again.

Cornelius also had a kindness deep inside him. His father often told him it was the one thing he inherited from his mother. When Cornelius was a boy, he'd finish working in his father's shop for the day and head over to the market to help his grandmother and her friends. One day while he was carrying some firewood on his shoulder for one of the women, two boys jumped up, grabbed the ends of a log, and just hung there. Cornelius laughed and slowly spun in a circle until the giggling boys finally dropped to the ground and stumbled off into the crowd. As a grown man, Cornelius often collected fruit from the merchants in the market and took it to the beggars who sat near the city gate.

One afternoon Cornelius stood in the cooking room of his small house, leaning against the table. His large hand worked at a piece of fruit. As he peeled, his daughter Rachel wandered into the room. She was four. In her arms she hugged a rag doll her mother had made for her. Rachel stood at his feet and looked up at him. She held out her arms.

Cornelius put the fruit aside and reached for her. Her tiny hands barely wrapped around his two fingers as he lifted her up and sat her on his arm. She leaned her face into his neck and yawned.

"Perhaps," said Cornelius, "you are like your father, and you would like some fruit. What do you think?" She nodded but didn't speak. "Would you like to be as big as your father when you grow up?" She giggled. This was her game. Sometimes she'd put on his helmet and march around the room. She'd poke him in the stomach with her finger, and he'd fall like Goliath slain by David.

Cornelius laid a massive hand on her back and held her close.

The knock at the door startled them both. Rachel could feel her father tense. She held her doll tighter. Cornelius kissed her and said, "Go in the other room with your mother." The girl didn't protest. She did as she was told and scooted off into the sleeping room.

When Cornelius opened the door, he was engulfed in light. It was a light that came at him like a wind and swirled around him. He tried to close his eyes against it but couldn't. Even so, it didn't occur to him to be afraid. He'd been a captain of the centurions for years. He sensed nothing menacing in this light. It embraced him like his daughter's hug.

"Cornelius," a voice said.

Cornelius saw a face, soft and feminine. The strands of her long, white hair disappeared, fading into the light around her as if she were standing in a breeze that Cornelius couldn't feel. The being reached out and placed a hand on Cornelius's cheek that gave him instant peace.

"I come with a message from God," the angel said. "He's a big fan."

Cornelius found he could say nothing. He could only be a part of the light.

"There is a man called Peter. He is a preacher. Do you know of him?"

Cornelius merely nodded. Everyone knew the crazy preacher who shouted his prayers in the markets. He was the only man Cornelius knew who laughed while he prayed.

Cornelius knew what had happened to the preacher's mentor. Cornelius had even heard Peter's mentor preach once. Caesar wasn't too happy about the preacher continuing to share his mentor's message. So the man called Peter moved around a lot. He stayed with various people to keep the authorities guessing as to where he'd turn up next.

The angel said, "Peter is staying with Simon the tanner whose house is in Joppa by the sea." The angel lightly brushed the hair from Cornelius' eyes. "God would like you to offer your hospitality to Peter for a little while. Send some of your men to collect him."

Cornelius was sure he'd done no more than blink. But when he opened his eyes, the angel was gone and so was the light. He now stood in front of a closed door. He shook his head in wonder and realized his hair had fallen into his eyes again.

Turning, Cornelius saw little Rachel at the door of the sleeping room, her eyes wide with surprise. "Did you see that?" Cornelius asked.

Rachel didn't speak or even blink, but she nodded.

Cornelius said, "Go get your mother."

Peter had taken to sleeping late. When he was a fisherman, he'd be up long before dawn. He figured if a man didn't see the sunrise from the water, then he'd wasted half his day. That was something his father used to say. But since Peter had gone into the full-time preaching business, everything had changed. Check that. Everything had pretty much changed from the moment Jesus said, "Come."

After Jesus' death Peter had gone back into fishing. There was something comforting about it. Ironically, it was the feel of the boat rocking beneath him that gave him a sense of stability. It was security. It was home. But then Jesus showed up again—after his death—and said Peter was going to be the start of something new and take over the ministry. He'd keep on doing the work they'd been doing for the last three years and make it grow.

Now Peter slept late. It was partly because Simon the tanner (at whose house he was now staying) worked well into the night and sang—badly—while he worked, and partly because Peter spent a great deal of time in other people's homes, telling them stories about Jesus and helping them see that this "new way" was *the* way. And it was partly—well, just because he could.

Peter opened his eyes as he lay on the sleeping mat. The room was small, but Simon had given it to him so he could be alone. Located at the top of the stairs, the room gave Peter private access to the roof, which is where he liked to pray. Peter loved Simon's house. It was by the sea, and Peter loved the sound and smell of the water. He felt connected to it.

It was nearly noon. Peter stood and scratched his belly. He washed his face in the bowl and then went out on the roof to pray.

Peter kneeled in prayer for the better part of an hour. But his concentration was eventually broken by the sound of his stomach rumbling. He stood and wondered if Simon's wife had begun to prepare lunch yet.

Then Peter became aware of the sudden stillness around him. The trees seemed to stop swaying. The sounds of the town over the hill had been silenced. He turned and looked out at the sea. It was as if the tide had stopped as well.

"Peter."

It was a quiet voice, but one he'd heard before. In fact, he'd been longing to hear it again.

"Yes, Lord." Peter said. He looked up and saw what he thought was a giant sheet—but it was larger than a house. It was big enough to serve as a tent over Caesar's palace. The sheet was being held at its four corners, and a massive weight inside the sheet appeared to be moving.

The corners of the sheet slowly opened, and inside it were hundreds upon hundreds of animals. There were lions and elephants and wolves. There were amazing creatures that Peter had once seen coming off a ship for the emperor's entertainment. There were bears and birds of all sizes. There were long snakes and bumpy lizards and giant turtles. There were even creatures that Peter had never dreamed of. There were birds with wingspans larger than a man. There were magnificent horses and cattle. There were pigs and chickens and apes. Peter wondered if this was what Noah saw. Then he wondered why God would show him such a vision.

From the center of the crowd of beasts—beasts that normally would have torn each other apart—an angel stepped forward. He was taller than Peter by four or five feet. His wings, though massive, where folded behind him. His hair hung in long spirals down past his shoulders. He patted an elephant on its side and smiled as he walked forward. When he got to the edge of the sheet, he drew a long hunting knife, larger than any knife Peter had ever seen. The angel deftly flipped the knife into the air and caught it by the blade. Then he held out the handle to Peter.

Peter heard the voice of God say, "Lunchtime."

Peter was appalled. Eat those animals? Was this a test?

He said, "Lord, I am a devout man. I keep your laws. So I won't eat what is unclean."

God's voice said, "Lunchtime. Go. Kill. Grill. And eat."

Peter was a hardcore Jew. He knew the laws. He knew which animals were unclean—an abomination. He'd memorized the laws of Leviticus long before any of his classmates had managed to. He knew what was good and proper. "I won't eat what is unclean," he repeated.

The angel's face didn't change, but the look in his eyes said, "Bad move."

The voice of God thundered, "Who are *you*? Who are you to say that anything—*anything* I made is unclean? Do you think I make mistakes? Do you think I'd make something that is beneath you? Unworthy of you? Is that what you think of your God and Creator?"

"But it's not kosher," Peter said.

"Nothing God makes is unclean," the voice said. "If God says you can eat, then eat."

Suddenly the sheet was pulled up by its corners, and Peter was shaken from his trance by a knock on the door. He looked over to see Simon's daughter standing there. She said, "Sir, there are three men here to see you."

Peter started for the door when the voice spoke to him once more. "Go with them."

So Peter traveled to the house of Cornelius. The giant of a centurion was standing at the door when he arrived.

"You won't believe what happened to me," they said to each other simultaneously.

RANDOM THOUGHTS ABOUT THE STORY OF CORNELIUS AND PETER

Isn't it interesting how so many of our great Bible heroes make the same mistakes—some of them again and again? They try to put a limit on God. God has no limits. God is so far beyond our imagination that we can't conceive of all that he is.

Look at the words below. Circle the one that you believe best connects you to God. Draw a square around the one that best connected you to God five or ten years ago.

Sight**Taste****Touch****Smell****Sound**

If someone told you that God usually shows up in the blank space, what do you think that means?

When Jesus first showed up, Peter was a fisherman named Simon, a man of the water. But just before Jesus left earth, he changed Simon's name to Peter, which means "rock."

Simon to Peter.

Water to Rock.

Draw a simple sketch of water washing up on a beach. In the water, draw a rock. Give the rock a name. Name it after the person who's your "rock," the one you can count on always to be there for you. Draw yourself on the beach, walking away from the water. In the space below, write down the most important lesson you learned from your "rock."

The first thing Jesus said to Peter was, "Follow me." The last thing Jesus said to Peter was, "Lead."

God brings us to him, turns our lives upside down, helps us get our footing again, and then asks us to put others through the same process.

God makes things happen. God starts the ball rolling. God puts us in front of each other so we have to work together to make wonderful things happen.

Peter was out on a roof wondering what God would ask him to do next. When he received his instructions, he questioned them. In those days a man like Peter wouldn't go to a place like Caesarea to speak to a man like Cornelius. It just wasn't done. God made sure that Peter looked past his rules and rule books.

God put Peter in front of a man who could take the gospel message to places where Peter couldn't go alone. Before this, Peter truly believed the gospel message was for his people (the Jews) and his people alone. God told him otherwise.

Think of a person you never expected to be a part of your life, but, as it turns out, became an incredibly significant part of it (even if it was only for a short time). Write the person's name here.

Even going to Cornelius' home was against the rules for a devout Jew like Peter. And Cornelius defied people's expectations about a Roman centurion. Neither Cornelius nor Peter fit anyone's mold as to what they should be like.

Everyone in your life is there for a reason. Yes, even that person. God sees what we can't see. God knows what we need. To say, "Uh...I think you've got this one wrong, God," is to put a limit on what God can do.

You can't limit the limitless. You can't put conditions on the unconditional. God doesn't play favorites. God doesn't hate. God doesn't hide.

Whoever you are, whatever your gifts may be, whatever your place—God can use you for his purposes. Open yourself up to that possibility, and God will put amazing people in front of you and show you incredible places.

THE STORY CONTINUES

Draw a picture of a T-shirt. On the front of it, write the word HERE. This week, as you go about your regular getting-ready-for-the-day routine, imagine yourself putting on this shirt. No one else knows you're wearing it. Imagine yourself saying, "I'm Here," to everyone you meet. See if it changes the way people react to you. Write down your thoughts at the end of the week.

BEZALEL

Based on Exodus 31:1-11

Moses stood outside the tent and took a deep breath. Then he took another. He'd been putting this off. He'd known Bezalel for years. He was a good man, but lately he'd simply been off his nut.

Moses had long ago stopped questioning why God did certain things. Why God did *anything* was pretty much a moot point because he never explained anything he didn't feel like explaining. If God wanted a portable church to be carried to each new spot, constructed, worshipped in, and then taken down and moved again, then *that* was exactly what God was going to have.

So God decided Bezalel was the man for the job. Moses knew Bezalel was a creative guy but nothing like this. Whenever you talked with Bezalel now, it was as if his mind was a million different places all at once. It was as if, in his mind, Bezalel wasn't just talking to you out in the desert; instead, he was in a palace with magnificent high arches. And everything Bezalel saw gave him ideas for 10 other things. His expertise in...well, just about *everything* had increased 10—no, 100 times over. He was a master of tapestry, carpentry, gold and silver, and even precious stones. If you found an interesting stone in the sand and gave it to Bezalel, later on you'd most likely discover it as part of an altar or threaded on a gold chain and hanging around some woman's neck.

What's more, the light inside of Bezalel was infectious. The men and women whom he called to work with him were always smiling, laughing for no reason, and singing songs as they worked. Moses hadn't felt that kind of joy in a long time. He'd taken to wearing the hood of his cloak down over his face so people wouldn't see that the light had gone out in him. Moses took one more deep breath and entered the tent.

"Moses!" Bezalel shouted almost immediately. He bounced over to the Israelite leader as though he'd been hitting the juniper berries since sunrise. He was halfway to Moses when he suddenly decided to do some kind of interpretive dance while he sang, "Moses! Moses! Moses!" The people around him began singing along as though they'd been rehearsing the tune for months. Bezalel did some sort of gliding leap that Moses guessed was either a depiction of

Pharaoh's guards drowning in the Red Sea or an indication that Bezalel had gotten his ephod in a bunch.

Bezalel embraced Moses as if they hadn't seen each other in years. (Moses guessed it was probably just since the breakfast manna.) "When are you going to let me sew you a new cloak?" Bezalel asked. "This one is getting kind of tattered."

"Well—"

"Oh, wait! You have to see this!" Bezalel said. He grabbed Moses by the front of his tunic and pulled him toward the back of the tent. A fire was burning, and a huge kettle sat on top of a stove that Bezalel had built around the flames. Moses could see they were melting gold. "We've been working on ways to slow the heating process."

"I see," Moses said, not sure what that had to do with anything.

"We can make it the consistency of cream. And then we can find all sorts of ways to mold it."

"Funny you should mention that," Moses said, happy to get five words said without being interrupted again. "He wants something else."

Bezalel stopped and stared at Moses with wide eyes. "Are you serious? He wants something more?" The smile that came to Bezalel's face nearly blinded Moses. Bezalel began to jump up and down with excitement. He spun around to face his workers and shouted, "Everyone! God wants something more!"

Everyone dropped what they were doing (except for the men working with the hot kettle full of melted gold, thankfully) and began hugging each other and dancing.

Moses felt another pang of jealousy. How long had it been since he'd danced at every new instruction from God?

"What does he want?" Bezalel asked excitedly. "More tapestry? Another altar?"

Moses looked his old friend in the eye and put his hands on Bezalel's shoulders to keep him from vibrating. "God wants a box," he said.

The change in Bezalel had happened six months earlier.

But Bezalel wasn't known as "Bezalel" back then. He was just "Uri's kid." And to most of the tribe—and a majority of his family—he might as well have been "Bezalel the Invisible."

Then it happened.

Bezalel had wandered off by himself...again. He'd taken to doing that more and more often, just to escape the sameness of his life. Every day he saw the same faces. Every day he ate the same food. Every day he saw the same scenery.

Bezalel enjoyed walking in the desert at night, where he could just stand and look at the stars. If he stared long enough, they shimmered. For years his people had been wandering. Yet nothing seemed to change except the stars. People got older and died and were replaced by people just like them. But the stars changed. The stellar patterns that Bezalel had learned as a boy spun in the night sky. It was a refreshing change from days that were frustratingly, agonizingly the same.

It's not that Bezalel wasn't grateful; he was. From the time he was very young, his grandfather Hur would tell him stories of the heartless Pharaoh they'd escaped. "Mean as a snake and twice as slithery" is how his grandpa had described him. And Hur was a great warrior. People from all over knew his name and accomplishments.

They also knew Bezalel's father, Uri, whose name meant "fire." Uri was one of the most feared gatekeepers of the tabernacle. Children referred to him as "the wall" because if he stood in the entrance, it was as if the wall of the tent had no opening. Bezalel's father filled the empty space.

"Who am *I*?" Bezalel would ask. In the desert he could say such things out loud. He could even shout it if he wanted to. The exodus was all he'd ever known—not to mention stories about Uri the Gatekeeper and Hur the Warrior.

"What am I?" Bezalel would ask the night—every night. He thought ruefully about the meaning of his own name: "In the shadow of God."

"In the shadow of 'the wall,' is more like it," Bezalel muttered.

He wandered far enough that he could see the lights of the camp in the distance, but no farther. This was all the farther he'd ever been from his people. He was just another wanderer. He was just another walker. He was just another face in a great line of disappointed and dejected faces.

Even Moses seemed a little darker these days. It was as if the light inside of him, which everyone wanted, was a little dimmer. His words were joyous and hopeful, but not so much the man who said them. People praised God when Moses spoke, but they did it in the way a person might say, "What a beautiful baby," about a child whose face could stop a toad in mid-jump. There was no genuineness in the words—no sincerity, no passion.

Even Bezalel's solitary walks had begun to lose their appeal. He found himself asking questions but receiving no answers. He no longer found comfort in the possibility that the answers were simply "out there" and would soon be revealed to him. There was just a lot of nothing.

Then Bezalel, son of Uri and grandson of Hur, pulled the hood of his cloak back from his head and looked directly up at the stars. He tried to see past the dark expanse, to catch a glimpse of the light beyond it. "Who am I?" he asked the sky. "I know who my grandfather is. I know who my father is. But what about me?"

Bezalel's frustration and anger and pain and disappointment welled up in his soul. He held out his arms and screamed at the sky, "WHO AM I?"

Suddenly Bezalel felt two giant, invisible hands grab him under the arms and lift him off the ground at a dizzying speed. His walking stick tumbled out of his hands, but he was too far up to hear it hit the sand. Bezalel was pulled toward the night sky he'd been screaming at only a moment before.

A blinding light poured over him. Its beams shot through his eyes and mouth and out his toes and fingers and the ends of his hair. Air rushed by his ears in a deafening roar. Bezalel couldn't hear his own scream. But it wasn't a scream of fear. Along with the light and the rush of air, he felt an overwhelming sense of safety, like he was being pulled into his mother's arms after a nightmare.

He wasn't aware that his ascent was slowing until he finally heard his own scream in his ears. The light dimmed and Bezalel found himself in front of a stained-glass window with great circular patterns that seemed to rotate upon themselves and radiate outward. Faces were etched in the glass. Light shone through them, bathing Bezalel in warmth and light. He didn't know the faces, but he felt a connection to them. He felt they were part of the family of God.

The hands that held Bezalel tossed him into the air the way a father tosses a giggling child. Bezalel felt himself being thrown toward a ceiling and nearly colliding with the face of God. God the powerful. God the ancient. God was painted on the ceiling of a magnificent structure, his long white hair and beard flowing behind him as he reached out to touch the finger of a man whose face Bezalel recognized. "Father Adam," Bezalel said.

The invisible hands spun him in a circle. Bezalel laughed. He knew he should be terrified, yet he was enveloped by a sense of love and safety.

Next he passed identical towers that scraped the sky, giant ornate statues, portraits of men and women in vibrant colors, and great buildings that seemed to wrap around themselves in diminishing circles.

Then the hands let him go. As Bezalel soared across the sky, he heard music—harmony, melody, and drums like he'd never heard before. He heard voices speaking in unfamiliar languages. But their message was obvious:

> God is good.
> God is love.
> God is all.
> God is here.
> God is there.
> God is within.
> God is without.

God is love.
God is love.
God is love.
It's a beautiful day.

The music drifted away, and Bezalel felt himself soaring like a rock skipping across the water. He landed in the sand and tumbled for what seemed like miles. When he finally rolled to a stop, he let his arms fall to his sides. His right hand landed on his walking stick.

"Ohhhhh, God," he prayed. "Ohhhhh myyyy, God."

Bezalel lay in the sand, his skin and muscles thrumming. When he closed his eyes, he could feel his eyeballs vibrating inside his lids.

"I guess that answers my question," he said and started to laugh.

RANDOM THOUGHTS ABOUT THE STORY OF BEZALEL

Of all the stories in this book, this one is the most dramatized. We know very little about Bezalel from Scripture. What we have to imagine is what it would be like to have God breathe into you—to actually have the Creator of the universe breathe into you and say, "Hang on, Sparky, here we go."

What does inspiration feel like for you?

Have you ever stood in the stands at a football game and "felt" something bigger than yourself? It's called school spirit: The connection of everyone in the stands as they cheer and sing and collectively run (in spirit) with their receiver down the field.

Have you ever walked into a room and sensed there was an argument going on just before you got there? You don't need to hear it. You *feel* it. The spirit of the room is angry.

It's been said that before he wrote a single note, Mozart could hear an entire symphony at once. He could see the notes all at one time, and then he'd hurry to write them down. Henry Ford would sit in his office for hours and stare at a blank wall, visualizing all the inner workings of his factory and his cars. Inspiration is the divine breath of God.

When you feel that spark—that moment—God is with you. You've made contact with the Spirit of God.

What is it that while you're doing it, you think, "I could do this forever"? Write it down here.

Saint Ignatius said that's where we meet God.

Maybe it's a song, a poem, a math equation, a football play, or a painting. Maybe you're not even trying that hard to be inspired when inspiration suddenly comes to you. What would happen if we learned to see those instances as God breathing into us?

The story of Bezalel is one of the first places in the Bible where it seems God breathed into a specific individual for a specific purpose—and it was an artist.

Not a minister, not a prophet, but an artist—the son and grandson of warriors.

God calls us all. His good grace calls us—not our parents, not our teachers, not even our youth ministers.

No one else can tell you what you're to become. That's entirely between you and God.

THE STORY CONTINUES

Look back at the list at the end of the story (the one that starts, "God is good"). Write your own list on the side of the page. Don't give it too much thought. Allow the Spirit to move you. There's no wrong answer. If you run out of space, use more paper or a handy napkin. Keep writing.